You Made My Day

Also by Janis Allen

Performance Teams: Completing the Feedback Loop

I Saw What You Did and I Know Who You Are:
Bloopers, Blunders, and Success Stories
on Giving and Receiving Recognition

(with Gail Snyder)

You Made My Day

Creating Co-Worker Recognition & Relationships

Janis Allen & Michael McCarthy

LEBHAR-FRIEDMAN BOOKS

New York • Chicago • Los Angeles • London • Paris • Tokyo

Lebhar-Friedman Books
425 Park Avenue
New York, NY 10022

Published by Lebhar-Friedman Books
Lebhar-Friedman Books is a company of Lebhar-Friedman, Inc.

Printed in the United States of America

Library of Congress Cataloging-in-Publication Data

Allen, Janis, 1950-
      You made my day: creating co-worker recognition and relationships / Janis
Allen and Michael McCarthy.
        p.   cm.
      Includes index.
      ISBN 0-86730-787-0
      1. Employee motivation. 2. Achievement motivation. 3. Social
acceptance. 4. Interpersonal relations.   I. McCarthy, Michael,
1948-   . II. Title.
HF5549.5.M63A53 2000
658.3' 14--dc21   99-30508
                                                                CIP

Book design, layout, and cover design by
Kathy Peterson of Advertising Plus.

Visit our Web site at lfbooks.com.

Dedicated

to

Pauline Allen
Gattis Ervin Allen
Laurel McCarthy
Johnny McCarthy

Acknowledging . . .

Theresa Chambers

Bradly Chapman

Don Ginder

Betsy Graham

Bernard Joseph

Russell Justice

Maria Kritzman

Melanie Lambert

Bill Lilly

Shawn McCarthy

Kay Reed

Gail Snyder

The contributions of these people
made this book what it is.

A Note to the Reader:

Part One of this book is designed for managers and supervisors but it should be read by everyone who wants to gain some insight into how a manager or supervisor can create a positive working environment. *Part Two* is for everyone who likes to learn and is willing to be a leader in making our daily lives more positive and productive.

A few words of explanation of how this book is written:

I means Janis. Michael's stories and material are written in third person and identified with his name. Although the book is co-authored, we thought it would be clearer to use one voice.

Male and female pronouns are used randomly.

We have found that the principles exposed in this book are universal and therefore work both at home and at work. We have included some "home and family" examples to give you an idea of what we mean. Based on our experience, if you practice these concepts at home, you are more likely to be comfortable doing it with co-workers.

Recognition and relationships are intertwined concepts that are difficult to separate. We find it to be similar to the poet William Butler Yeats's observation, "How do you tell the dancer from the dance?" We often can't tell the relationship from the recognition. A relationship is composed of the feelings created by past actions and words between two people. Recognition is showing how you value another person's work. Recognition (giving and receiving) is difficult or impossible when competitiveness, lack of trust, or insensitivity are part of the way people relate.

Although this book is copyrighted, we have designated pages that may be copied for your use.

For a good time . . . turn to the back of the book and read the subject index first. Michael created it, and it's unique. It'll have you dying to read the rest of the book.

CONTENTS

PART ONE:

RECOGNITION AND PERFORMANCE

PART TWO:

CO-WORKER RECOGNITION AND RELATIONSHIPS

PART ONE

RECOGNITION
AND PERFORMANCE

The Relationship Between Recognition & Performance

~1~
CO-WORKER RECOGNITION AND RELATIONSHIPS

When I was eleven, I cut the grass in my family's yard all by myself for the first time. I was tired, but, oh, so proud.

A family friend drove into the driveway just as I was finishing. His first words out of the car were "You missed a spot behind the shrubs." I was crushed. Why hadn't he noticed the rest of the four acres that I had mowed correctly with so much sweat and effort? I suppose his eye was trained to look for the imperfect spot. I never wanted to cut the grass again.

Most of us know the power of other people's approval or disapproval in motivating us to keep trying—or throw in the towel. A smile and a comment that shows someone values our efforts will keep us going for a long time.

Joanna Solfrain, a sales and marketing assistant at *Drug Store News*, told me about a week when her supervisor was out of town, and she had been working through lunches and until seven P.M. every night to meet department deadlines. She was feeling burned out, she said, when Wayne, a co-worker, came and stood for a minute at her cubicle door one evening watching her work. "You work hard," he said quietly, and then turned back to his work.

"Those three words kept me going for three more days," Joanna said. "Wayne is a man who doesn't mince words, so I was quite positive that his comment was genuine. In my boss's absence, someone recognized my work."

Historically, we've expected managers and supervisors to provide the positive recognition for the people who work for them. Or, worse, we've depended on merit pay raises, end-of-project celebrations, or annual appraisals to motivate people.

"There's nothing wrong with any of the things listed above," Dr. Aubrey Daniels, author of *Bringing Out the Best in People* and a pioneer in the field of performance improvement, notes. "They're just too little, too late."

Now is a time when many of us who are non-supervisors are ready and willing to take more of a leadership role than ever in managing our own careers and work experiences. We want to take positive steps to support the good performance of our teammates, all in the name of creating the best products, the best customer service, and a good place to work. Everyone likes to get recognition. When a co-worker notices what I do, I make double sure that I continue to do it.

CO-WORKER RECOGNITION: Melanie Lambert, IBM

"Monique, a human-resources professional, joined IBM during the implementation of a high-profile and critical program. As a new employee, she didn't know a lot about the program or our organization, but that didn't slow her down a bit. She jumped right in and quickly got herself up to speed. She worked hard, offered creative ideas, and became sought out by her teammates and managers.

"No sooner did this first key project end than Monique was asked to help another department. She rolled up her sleeves and learned

—*continued on next page*

everything she could about their business. She then took the lead in creating a staffing and recruiting plan.

"Only nine months after starting with the company, Monique was nominated by her co-workers for IBM's 'Passion for Business' award. That was ironic because it was Monique herself who was responsible for giving this award to other employees. This time we had to pretend that someone else was being honored."

The comments written to nominate Monique included:

- *"She demonstrates boundless enthusiasm."*
- *"She never talks about what she's doing or the long hours she's working. She just gets things done—with a smile."*
- *"She's not looking for recognition—she's looking for ways to contribute."*
- *"People want to be like Monique."*
- *"She sets the standard."*

"When those comments were read at our holiday gathering," Melanie said, "Monique was flabbergasted and thrilled. Because this award allows us to recognize our peers, it generates a lot of excitement and encourages ongoing passion for our business!"

My dad fought in the Pacific during World War II. When veterans of this war were asked what they were proudest of in their lives, most of them described events during battles in which their lives were threatened or when they struggled to save their own lives or those of their buddies. Who could imagine a worse situation to be in? Yet, those soldiers felt good telling their stories. When asked why, one responded, "I knew that what I was doing was valuable."

Value is an important theme throughout our daily lives. The power of recognition is as simple as this: When someone comments favorably on my work, I know it's valuable.

We all are proud of the value we create, and we feel good when someone else can also see value in it. The validation adds to our sense of accomplishment.

Some people know the value of their efforts

"I knew that what I was doing was valuable."

without being told. They are the people we call self-motivated, and we love to have them as co-workers.

Kirsten was elected by her fellow teachers as the best educator in the school. She felt so honored to know that her co-workers valued her work. Kirsten had been brave enough to pioneer the new "Self-contained Special Education" methodology at the school, combining sixth, seventh, and eighth graders with learning disabilities into one classroom.

Then she attended a luncheon with teachers from other schools. In conversation, she discovered that all the others had been selected by their supervisors to attend as "best teacher," but none of them knew specifically why they had been selected or who had made the choice. Their comments about being chosen were cynical and mocking. They enjoyed the food, but they regarded the recognition as a joke. Kirsten privately knew that her peers recognized her for pioneering and succeeding with the new format, but the luncheon was kind of a downer for her. The best feeling had been the one she'd had *before* the lunch: the pride in her colleagues' respect for her work.

Some people may say that the only important recognition comes from the boss, the person who has the power to write our evaluations or give us a promotion or pay raise. But many of us underestimate the nonmonetary value of the approval of our co-workers.

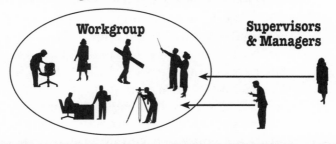

Recognition from Outside the Circle

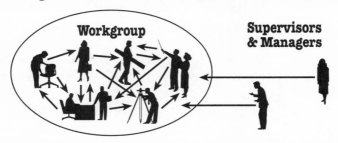

Recognition from Inside _and_ Outside the Circle

INSIDE THE CIRCLE: Russell Justice, Eastman Chemical

"Inside this circle is a group of people who work together. The supervisor and managers are the figures just outside the circle. The rate of performance improvement inside the circle is directly related to the amount of positive recognition that can be pumped into the circle.

"If we depend on all recognition to come from outside the circle, it will be limited and late. These supervisors and managers can't possibly see all the productive actions and performance improvements as they happen. But the people inside the circle can spot most of them.

"It's everyone's job to give positive recognition to the people who are helping them get their jobs done.

"When my boss tells me I've done a good job training people, I like to hear it. How does he know, though? He knows if one of my customers or one of my colleagues tells him. On the other hand, when I'm team-teaching with a colleague, he or she knows first-hand. I admit that when my supervisor comments positively about my work, part of me is thinking, 'If you only knew how hard this job is.' My colleagues know, because they are living it."

We can't change other people. We can only change ourselves.

Giving recognition to our co-workers adds value to both the self-motivated and the not-so-self-motivated among us. It's icing on the cake for the people performing so well that we have to chase them down to tell them we like their work.

Not everyone will respond to our positive recognition as we would like. Trial and error is instructive. I once made a positive comment about a colleague's teaching style and he frowned, made a spitting noise and stomped off. But don't let it frustrate you when you don't get the reaction you want. Give your recognition, and let go of it. We can't make other people change; we can change only ourselves. As we change our own behavior toward people in our lives, it often influences them to change.

Most of us appreciate it when someone unexpectedly stops taking our work for granted and gives it a little positive attention.

Throughout this book, we will give you insights about how to give recognition effectively to co-workers, how to avoid minefields, and how to create healthy working relationships that make positive recognition the icing on the cake.

Here's an E-mail to a co-worker that supports good customer service *and* values her colleague's actions:

> ANTOINETTE,

> Not that I'm eavesdropping, but I often hear
> you on the phone with clients since you are right
> opposite my wall. It dawned on me today, when
> I took a moment to really listen to you, that you
> are very courteous and well-spoken, and have a
> very relaxed and yet helpful demeanor toward
> your clients. I think that you should feel good to
> know that not everyone handles clients that well,
> and that consequently, it makes you exceptional
> that you handle things the way you do. Whatever
> you do, don't change that. I know from my own
> experience that having a pleasant voice at the
> other end of the phone can make doing business
> so much easier and more comfortable.

> Sincerely,

> David

TRY IT OUT!

As a private exercise, think of your last two workdays. Who has performed activities that helped you succeed and what were they?

WHO	WHAT

Whether you mention anything to these people is up to you. Practice noticing the helpful actions of your co-workers. Make copies of this page and practice every day for a week if you like.

~ 2 ~
NICE IS NICE: POSITIVE RECOGNITION IS SOMETHING DIFFERENT

Positive recognition is different from "being nice"—not that there's anything wrong with being nice.

People sometimes tell me, "Positive recognition is my natural style. I always say 'Good morning,' I send birthday cards, and I help people when they need it." Those are all nice ways to treat people, but positive recognition is different. Positive recognition is pointing out a specific behavior that you like in a person and then telling that person what you like about it. It's a reaction from you that follows a particular behavior or celebrates its results.

Niceness is free; recognition is earned.

The following note is a perfect example of naming something specific a co-worker did, which in turn gives her positive recognition.

Jessica:

I just wanted to thank you for helping me out last week. By keying in those two items for "Supply Side" and helping me with the transcription of Marie's tape, I was able to tackle some of the other projects I had piled up on my desk. I really appreciate it!!!

—Cheryl

Catch someone doing something right.

II

The Relationship Between Management Recognition & Co-worker Recognition

~ 3 ~
WHY RECOGNIZE CO-WORKERS?

Who cares about receiving attention from co-workers?

Fred, a mechanical engineer, did not believe in recognition. His philosophy was, "I should do my work and get paid, and that's it." Fred was assigned a very high-profile design project that required much work. His task was to rearrange the assembly line for large tractors. Fred had to create a plan for closing down the old line and starting up his newly-designed line. Two challenges loomed:

- Meeting a tight schedule
- Shutting down the old and starting up the new without losing production

If he didn't succeed, a costly shutdown would occur, losing money for the company and failing to satisfy customer orders.

The heat was on. Fred was a proud engineer who never asked anyone for help. He worked feverishly to meet the deadline, working countless evening hours. Soon, though, it became apparent that he was not going to be able to complete the project on time.

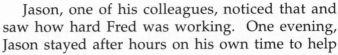

Jason, one of his colleagues, noticed that and saw how hard Fred was working. One evening, Jason stayed after hours on his own time to help Fred. Then he stayed another evening and another. After several nights of working together, Fred and Jason completed the project just in time.

Fred was relieved and so appreciative that someone would give up his free time to assist him. He asked his supervisor how he could give Jason some recognition. Fred was given the time to stand up in a meeting and tell their peer group exactly what Jason had done, including how many hours he generously had given.

Little did Fred know that Jason had also secretly asked for time on the agenda to recognize Fred's work. After hearing Fred's words, Jason turned around and told the other engineers how diligently Fred had worked to meet the deadline and do it correctly. Fred's design would make a smooth transition from the old assembly line to the new, Jason declared.

Fred was speechless. He couldn't believe that he found himself on the receiving end of recognition before his peers, when all his focus had been on praising Jason for his unselfish help. Fred's face lit up, and it was an emotional moment for everyone in the room. Although Fred had always made it known that he didn't believe in recognition, everyone in the department witnessed a change of heart that day.

Needless to say, Fred is now a strong proponent of co-worker recognition and is good at receiving as well as giving.

Some people may feel reluctant to give recognition to co-workers, believing that their opinions don't matter. But many people tell me that they value it—and that it feels different from management recognition for several reasons:

- First, people we work with usually know our jobs much better than our bosses do, so they

can appreciate what it takes to achieve results.
- Next, there's no reason to question the sincerity of a work pal's positive comments. Unfortunately, some managers' positive recognition might be attributed to reasons like, "It's just the politically correct thing for managers to do," or "Wonder what she wants from me now?"
- Finally, recognition from co-workers makes us feel like a member of the team.

Some people may assume recognition to be a responsibility of only supervisors and managers. If you think of recognition as limited to promotions, awards, and banquets, that would be true.

The most meaningful recognition doesn't cost a dime. It's the attention we receive when another person pauses to tell us she sees value in the work we've done or the help we gave. Time is the most valuable commodity we human beings have. When we give a little of it to co-workers, they get the message that they are appreciated. As Theresa Chambers from the City Government of Seattle says, "Recognition isn't an item, it's an action."

A positive word about my performance from a colleague has another positive side effect too. It tells me that this person feels no need to compete with me or compare my work to hers. It sends the message that she is happy that I perform well and is willing to celebrate my good work. We are teammates. That is the icing on this cake: a trusting working relationship built by words of positive recognition.

Trust takes time and positive experience.

Recognition isn't an item; it's an action.
—*Theresa Chambers*

"THERE'S NO PRESENT LIKE YOUR TIME"

III

The Leverage Effect of Co-worker Recognition

~ 4 ~
MORE IS MORE

Anything that increases the amount of positive recognition for productive behavior is a good thing. When people who work together take the time to notice each other's contributions and make their awareness noticed, they create at least ten times more recognition than would be given if they waited for a supervisor or customer to do it.

Imagine a day like this: Edna walks by and sees the new chart you've printed for the staff meeting. "Wow! Neat chart," she observes. At the coffee pot, David says, "Hey, that estimate you sent me went into the Jones proposal. Perfect." Your E-mail contains a note from Jessie on your project team thanking you for taking the new team member to lunch. When you show your latest cost analysis to your teammate, she notices and comments that she likes the way you constructed your spreadsheet to roll up the quarterly figures.

A day like this contains more goodness than your boss has been able to notice in a month.

Such scenes make clear the other advantage of peer recognition—that it can happen so much more quickly and naturally than waiting for a manager to discover what deserves attention. If I work near

. . . a series of mini-recognition breaks to fuel your fire 'til quittin' time.

Notice good work and . . . make your notice noticed.

you, I can pause with a smile over a spreadsheet you've just created, nod while you tell me of a cost-saving idea, or read a great paragraph you've just written. That gives you a series of mini-recognition breaks that fuel your fire until quitting time.

We notice our co-workers' good work many times a day. But do they know that we noticed?

When Beethoven's "Ninth Symphony" was performed for its first time, the audience leapt to their feet with thunderous applause. Beethoven, who was deaf at that point in his life, had been conducting the orchestra himself. He stood expressionless with his back to the audience, still facing the orchestra. One of the musicians realized that Beethoven could not hear the applause, so he took the composer by the shoulders, and turned him around so he could see the hundreds of people on their feet, applauding.

Applause is certainly positive recognition—but not unless we know it's there. Don't assume your co-workers know how you feel about their work. In other words: Notice good work and . . . make your notice noticed.

TRY IT OUT!

Copy this page and write positive recognition notes to:

- a co-worker
- your supervisor
- your internal supplier
- your internal customer

👍 TO: _____

I like what you did . . .

_____

_____

_____

_____

_____

_____

Signed:_____

👍 TO: _____

I like what you did . . .

_____

_____

_____

_____

_____

_____

Signed:_____

Recognition
gives people
permission
to be proud
of what
they do.

The Proof Is in the Performance

IV.

~5~
HOW MANAGERS CAN CREATE THE ENVIRONMENT TO IMPROVE PERFORMANCE

At a manufacturing plant where I was personnel manager, the employee turnover was so high one year that we briefly considered giving gold watches for two weeks of service. That was crazy, but we were desperate. With 213 percent annualized turnover, it was equal to replacing every person on every job in the plant more than twice that year. We had tried the buddy system, a program to pair up new people with veteran employees, but the "veterans" averaged only four months on the job themselves. We tried paying a cash bounty to people who would refer a new employee who stayed sixty days. We tried having two company picnics a year instead of one.

We had the "doubling disease." Whatever wasn't working, we doubled it. It didn't work. Managers and supervisors became frustrated. How could they run the plant and be accountable for production quotas when they spent all their time interviewing, training, and literally running the open jobs themselves? Managers and supervisors began bailing

The "doubling disease."

22

out under the pressure too. Salaried employee turnover shot up to 62 percent.

Finally, having exhausted all the quick fixes, we (exhausted) managers tried an unquick fix. We began sharing individual and team production and quality performance with the people operating the machines by using two methods of feedback.

Supervisors privately reviewed each machine operator's previous-day performance with him or her at the beginning of the day, and offered coaching on how to improve if needed. They made positive comments to the operators when even small improvement was shown from the previous level, or when they maintained an improvement at the same level.

In addition, graphs illustrating team production and quality were posted near the break areas. Supervisors and department managers wrote short positive comments, or drew "smiley" faces or stars next to data showing improvement or gain maintenance.

Sounds almost childish and certainly simple. Surprise. It worked. Not only did the production rise to meet the plant production goal, but the percent of off-quality production dropped concurrently. Best of all, turnover was cut from 213 percent to 42 percent during the following twelve months. Those performance feedback practices were continued faithfully on a daily basis with the operators, and the lower turnover was maintained at 42 percent the second year.

All gimmicks aside, the new employees had begun to receive more accountability and positive attention for their machine efficiency and quality. It

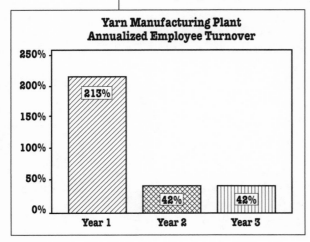

**Yarn Manufacturing Plant
Annualized Employee Turnover**

was the first management practice that worked and was sustained over time, and it made a believer out of me. As a result, I have spent the rest of my career helping managers to replicate that kind of experience.

What has changed over this period? Just one important addition. We have learned that "top-down" performance feedback and recognition is only one significant source and a small percentage of what's valuable.

In my last ten years of working with organizations, I have encouraged them to use 80 percent of their training and coaching resources with employees instead of with managers and supervisors. We teach them to develop measures, goals, and daily feedback tools for their own performance. They learn how to notice positive performance and behaviors of their co-workers, and to give positive attention to these things. In those ten years, not a single employee has said to me, "This is not my job." They have told me, "I think my boss should be doing this." That, of course, is true, and means that the supervisors and managers should be using positive feedback and recognition practices before they expect their teams to do likewise.

"Top-down" feedback and recognition are only a part of what's valuable to employees.

Results in Engineering Design

At Emerson Electric in Orlando, Florida, an engineering design team was challenged to design a radar indicator for U.S. Navy aircraft with a smaller budget than they had projected, and to deliver the quality-tested prototype four months earlier than they had been able to produce a similar piece of equipment.

Eddie Brewer, the group leader, tried some new procedures. Representatives of the manufacturing department were asked to join the design team so that their input on "what's possible" could be considered during the initial stages of design, rather than wait until the end of the design phase, as had previously been done.

The entire team was given the budget and timetable goals that were in the government contract, and asked to work on new methods for meeting them.

The team was given training in goal-setting, frequent visual feedback, and positive recognition methods for team members to use with each other. Every two weeks, the team met for thirty minutes to review the progress on action items from the last meeting. Individuals who had met their goals were given positive comments, high-fives, and applause by the group. During those meetings the group also brainstormed lists of day-to-day productive behaviors and posted them to remind everyone what to look for and to make positive comments to their co-workers.

The team leader surprised the group with a lunch when milestones were met.

When the design was completed and the tested prototype was delivered to the U.S. Navy, it met specifications on the first test—the first time this had been achieved. It was also 10 percent under budget and was delivered on schedule.

A "side-effect" mentioned by the team members was that they had learned more about the total project requirements as a result of combining the design and manufacturing teams and as a result of consciously looking for team member behaviors to recognize. The project was completed in a positive atmosphere, in which individuals were winners when they helped make the team win. Blaming others for mistakes, competition, and negative comments between design and manufacturing disappeared.

Results in Government Service

In 1993, Lt. Gov. Stan Lundine of New York challenged the state's Department of Motor Vehicles to improve its service to the citizens with the following statement: "Waiting in line for a driver's license is an aggravation nobody needs. People who wait in line one hour for a license that's good for four years often feel like they're waiting in line four years for a license that's good for one hour."

So Mike Losinger, deputy commissioner for DMV Operations, decided to do something about it. He and his management team embarked on a mission to reduce the time citizens were spending in DMV offices.

At twenty-five DMV offices in the state, teams of hourly associates and supervisors met to explore ways to improve their current processes for licenses and vehicle registrations. After agreeing on the changes they would make, they listed these actions in three categories:

- Managers' actions
- Supervisors' actions
- Associates' actions

They then posted them in the offices to:

- remind people to do these actions
- remind everyone to make positive comments to each other when they "caught" anyone doing these actions

In addition, they measured the average waiting time of people entering their offices and posted the data on a chart in the break room. As they proceeded with the improvements, they continued to measure and post the wait time. The charts demonstrated the lower waiting times over three months.

At the DMV office in Manhattan, they discovered that their historical customer wait

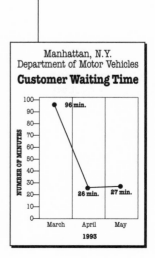

time was ninety-six minutes. When they posted the data and implemented their process changes, the wait time was reduced to twenty-six minutes the first month and leveled off at twenty-seven minutes in the second month.

They were proud of their improvements. On a bulletin board in the break area, they began posting positive recognition notes to each other, to let co-workers know they noticed the efforts they made in implementing the new processes. The bulletin boards filled up with positive notes and had to be cleared periodically to make room for new ones.

Of the twenty-five offices who participated, twenty-three reduced their customer wait time.

Results in Manufacturing

According to *Performance Management Magazine,* 3M Dental Products Manufacturing in Irvine, California, created a goal of implementing performance improvements using a baseball-themed point system and feedback bulletin board with positive recognition for managers and their teams. In six months, they documented $500,000 in savings.

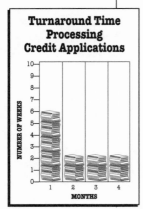

Pittsburgh Plate Glass in Lexington, North Carolina, used goals, feedback, and recognition to reduce plant safety incidents from 17 annually to 7.9.

Turnaround Time Processing Credit Applications

Results in Administrative Functions

Western Michigan University had a backlog of two thousand student credit applications. Overtime hours were costing the department money, and morale was sinking with this paper jam. The University set up individual goals, daily feedback, and positive recognition, and dug out from under the piles of paper. Application turnaround time was slashed from six weeks to two weeks and maintained.

Morale improved, overtime went to zero, and the managers were able to take their success to other universities to help with speedier turnarounds.

Results in Sales

In *How to Improve Human Performance*, Thomas Connellan documents how a wholesale distributor's inside sales department increased sales. The average number of line items per order was six, and the company wanted to increase this figure. Salespeople were given workshop training in sales techniques, and each wrote an action plan. Individuals set targets for improvement and tracked their own performance daily. Managers were instructed to talk with them weekly. They were trained to offer help by saying, "Is there anything else I can do to help you keep up your progress?" and to give each person positive recognition for any improvement, or just for maintaining the last week's improvement.

Managers' previous responses would have typically been to ignore improvement and grumble about employees who weren't "motivated" or "dedicated," or to chew out the salespeople who didn't meet their targets.

The new approach produced results. Within five weeks, the average line items per order increased from six to eleven.

These practices sound simple, and they are. But they require consistent application. The more people in an organization use them, the better your results will be, since employees come in contact with not just one supervisor but with employees, supervisors, and managers from many departments. The use of goals, daily and weekly feedback, and, most important, positive recognition, not only will improve performance, but it also will transform your culture.

Give recognition for maintaining last week's improvement.

V

The Manager's Roles and Responsibilities

~ 6 ~
CREATING A CO-WORKER RECOGNITION CULTURE

In the previous section, you read that the number-one role for managers and supervisors in promoting a co-worker recognition culture begins with "you first."

It would look pretty ridiculous for a supervisor to expect employees to give kudos to co-workers if the employees have to dodge beatings from them in order to do it. In addition to creating a positive working environment, other actions can be taken by managers to set up employees for success.

Setting Up the Environment: Using Data, Goals, Feedback, and Positive Recognition

Share performance data frequently. Educate people on their performance level. Let them know what you and customers expect.

Teach people how to set realistic but challenging goals, and make them public.

Coach your associates to set individual goals that show improvement from their own historical performances. Individual goals won't all be the same. Prepare yourself

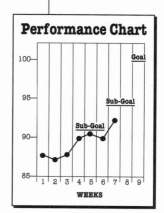

and co-workers to recognize improvement, even of low performers.

Post team or group performance data in a public place. Plot it on a graph. People won't take time to study numerical reports. Limit it to data that people have control over improving, such as team production and department turnaround times, sales, and quality. Never post individual performance; it sets people up for comparisons and stack-rankings, not recognition of how improvement was gained by all. In other words, don't just post company profit data or the stock price, and think that every employee knows how his actions on Tuesday at three P.M. affect it.

Celebrate when the data shows improvement! "Celebrate" can be done in many ways:

- Go to the individual's work area, and congratulate her for this week's improvement in her customer service.
- Gather the team around the graph, tell them you're proud that they maintained the gain they made two weeks ago, and invite them to talk about how they made it happen two weeks running. Your job is to keep the discussion on the subject of celebrating and recognizing the behaviors that "got us here and will keep us here." Don't allow negative talk to develop. You should open the discussion by naming the behaviors you've noticed that created the success and the people responsible.
- Visit employees to tell them what they did that helped contain costs.

Shut up as soon as you finish applauding.

Food and drink are always welcome but never required for positive recognition to be effective. The most important gift you give is your positive attention to their positive behaviors.

Let your positive recognition stand alone. In other words, *shut up as soon as you finish applauding.* The recipient of your recognition may respond by telling you some details about her work, and you will thus learn even more about how she succeeded.

This is not a time to give instructions for a new task, set higher goals, or assign additional work. Do those things at another time. You must let them savor your positive words without rushing to the next goal or cluttering up their good-feeling landscape with thoughts of the next project.

Leadership Through Example

Make positive statements. Michael tells about the first time he met Orelia Rogers, the vice president of purchasing for a trucking company. She had asked him and another colleague to help her implement a new process that would improve service to vendors.

Michael remembers quickly becoming enthusiastic about helping her. In fact, it was the end of the workday, and he had an appointment away from the office, but he became so interested in their discussion, he decided to cancel his appointment and keep working.

Why? He identified two of Orelia's behaviors that "hooked" him.

As she began brainstorming ways to tackle the project, she talked in positives about other people who could help: "I'll ask Joe to join our team. He's really resourceful at finding shortcuts that work without sacrificing quality. And Mary, she's great at getting things done quickly."

Orelia was a leader by taking action herself. She named some things she would do to get it rolling.

Those were two positive leadership behaviors that created enthusiasm immediately in Michael. They made him *want* to stay at work when it was time to leave.

... positive leadership behaviors made him *want* to stay at work when it was time to leave.

This chapter has been a short outline of performance leadership. You've seen most of the elements of performance improvement: measurement, feedback, and recognition. I don't expect you to use these tools perfectly, and neither will your employees. But the important thing is that they see you making the effort.

Seeing your willingness to change will go far in inciting and exciting them to want to change. If you take the leadership of acting first, you set the stage for a more positive and productive culture.

Maintaining the Gains:
How to Support These Practices

The remainder of this book is for co-workers. When you spot them engaging in co-worker recognition, quietly let them know that you noticed and that you appreciate their efforts.

Make a place at the beginning of your meeting agenda to go around the table and mention the contributions of fellow team members. Remember, you go first. Then reinforce others who join by listening and giving eye contact, and abstain from elaborating so much that you steal their spotlight.

Like you, your employees won't execute perfectly all the time, but if you show that you value their attempts, you will make huge strides together.

PART TWO

CO-WORKER
RECOGNITION
AND
RELATIONSHIPS

VI

Benefits for You and Your Co-workers

~ 7 ~
CREATING A POSITIVE CULTURE

"It is a good thing to hang an admiral from time to time, to encourage the others," said Voltaire in *Candide* after the English Royal Navy hanged Admiral Byng for losing a battle in 1756. Some encouragement! Some of us remember the old days in business when people were punished, which served as a fear-producing threat to others, lest they slack off.

Happily, many organizations now realize that actions like punishment only encourage people to hide mistakes, look for someone else to blame for problems, or only do enough to get by.

Richard had just returned to work at a company that works daily at giving positive recognition to associates. He said that he had stayed in contact with his friend Barbara since he left the company twelve years ago. She recently told him that it was now a much more enjoyable place to work. Trusting her to give him the straight "skinny," he left his other job and came back. Benefit: Attracting and re-attracting good people to work on your team.

Managers help set the tone for a positive work culture, but the day-to-day interactions with co-workers can make or break how your day goes.

The days of waiting for management to do something are over. You can improve working relationships, initiate teamwork, and give recognition to deserving associates with little or no involvement by the bosses.

The following are some examples of E-mail notes sent from one co-worker to another:

```
FROM:    Elledge, Joyce
SENT:    Friday, September 04, 1998
         12:10 PM
TO:      Collins, Marilyn
SUBJECT: ORDERS
```

Just wanted to let you know that we appreciate all you do to make our job so much easier. The care you take to prepare your orders shows that you have respect for your fellow employees and most of all your customers. It's nice to see that you have so much PRIDE in what you do. Thanks again for all your good efforts.

–Joyce

```
FROM:    Johnson, Denise
SENT:    Wednesday, September 30, 1998  5:43 PM
TO:      Figueroa, Sandra
SUBJECT: COMMUNICATION
```

NO PROBLEMS . . . NO QUESTIONS . . . I JUST WANTED TO TAKE TIME OUT TO SAY THANK YOU FOR SHARING YOUR KNOWLEDGE, YOUR PATIENCE, AND POSITIVE ATTITUDE. WE HAVE ESTABLISHED A LEVEL IN COMMUNICATION WHERE WE PREVENT ERRORS THAT COULD POTENTIALLY COST US! YOU ARE A PLEASURE TO WORK WITH AND I LOOK FORWARD TO COMING TO N.Y. AND MEETING YOU AND THE REST OF THE STAFF!

NIECY JOHNSON

Dave Haigh, from the Department of Housing and Human Services, City of Seattle, describes one method his department uses to create a positive culture:

"Managers and employees thank each other daily in their business interactions, but often co-workers are left out of the loop. So we've created a venue on the E-mail system called Kudos. Kudos is an E-mail bulletin board that is an easy way for all employees, regardless of their position in the organization, to recognize each other for good work."

Don Ginder of Delta Faucet describes success in changing a negative culture into a positive one:

"During a messy period of remodeling the offices of the sales and marketing department, we temporarily relocated twenty people into a half-court gym. They were shoulder-to-shoulder without enough room to set up all their office equipment conveniently. Dust and short tempers floated like pollution in the air. We introduced a fun process that some people didn't like at first. We made a small bulletin board for each person and hung it on his wall.

"Then, borrowing an idea from Aubrey Daniels & Associates, a performance management consulting team, we asked each person to select a type of sticker from rolls of different designs: animals, symbols, all kinds of fun cartoonish stickers. A sticker was placed at the top of each person's small bulletin board to show his personal sticker or symbol. Co-workers were asked to write a short recognition note to each other as follows:

To:_____

For: (naming the specific behavior) _____

_____

"They gave these notes to the co-worker they wanted to recognize and then placed one of their own stickers on that person's bulletin board.

"This process fed on itself. Pretty soon, even the naysayers were yaysayers. Those twenty people became happy, if still 'homeless'," Don concluded.

Think of recognition like the coins in the dishes we see at many cash registers:

GOT SOME RECOGNITION?
LEAVE SOME.

NEED SOME RECOGNITION?
TAKE SOME.

VII

Recognition: Builder of Positive Relationships

~ 8 ~
CELEBRATING OTHERS' SUCCESS

Jessica once worked in a marketing department for a supervisor who was jealous of the design department. Among other reasons, the supervisor resented the design people because they were able to leave the office at five P.M. every day. The supervisor worked until eleven P.M. most nights because she was disorganized and allowed so many interruptions during the day.

When Jessica needed to interact with "the enemy"—people on the design staff—and did it in a friendly way, the supervisor disapproved. She looked at Jessica resentfully while glancing at the design people with a frown on her face. She discouraged Jessica from informing them of changes early in the process or laughing and joking with them.

Sounds like the supervisor could leave at five o'clock every day if she had spent more time focusing on her own work rather than worrying about her staff's interactions with the design folks. Even though Jessica had positive relationships with both her boss and with her neighboring department, she felt the strain of her boss's petty remarks and jealousy.

> "Happiness is a perfume you cannot pour on others without getting a few drops on yourself."
>
> —Ralph Waldo Emerson

"We have met the enemy, and he is us."

—Pogo

Many of the relationship problems among co-workers stem from what I will call sibling rivalry. Just as small children in any family insist that no brother or sister be given a larger piece of cake, some people take these same jealous feelings into adulthood and into their jobs.

Unlike a layer cake, where more for you means less for me, there is no fixed amount of success that can be enjoyed at work. Certainly, Jessica's supervisor wasn't "losing" the right to complete her work and go home at five o'clock because the design folks had "won" the only "leave-work-at-five" prize. Since most of us grow up with competition and contests as the measure of success, we are trained from childhood to assume that every challenging situation must have a winner who takes all. We pour energy into worrying about our inability to grab the prize. We assume that there's only one prize. If organizations set up one-winner contests, or give recognition to only the top producers, this "limited pie" situation is perpetuated. That feeling makes it difficult to be happy for someone else's success.

When we open our eyes and see that there's enough recognition, enough places of success for all who will create it for themselves, we can relax and be generous with our recognition.

1998 will always be remembered for the surprising way that baseball players Mark McGwire and Sammy Sosa handled their relationship in the race for the single-season home-run record. We rarely see a baseball player congratulate another when his competitor pulls ahead in the competition. The good feelings those two mature people demonstrated for each other made fans admire them more. They will both have a unique place in sports history, and the images of Sosa

"WE LIKED WHAT YOU DID!"

hugging McGwire when McGwire broke Roger Maris's record is indelible to all of us who witnessed it.

★ SHARING THE STAGE ★

~9~
SHARING THE STAGE

At the Grand Ole Opry years ago, legendary singers Roy Acuff and Porter Wagoner were among those who sang to the audience. I couldn't help noticing how often those famous performers took time out from their songs to name the people who:

- had written the songs they were singing
- had first recorded the song
- were newcomers to the Opry stage
- were singing in their backup groups
- were playing in their bands

The schedule allowed fifteen minutes for each performer that day. This scarcity of stage time made it even more surprising that these veterans were willing to give their time to singers who were much less famous. They seemed not to fear losing something when a competitor gained something. They acted as if there was enough out there to go around for everyone—enough public attention, enough good songs, enough customers, enough record producers, enough fans, enough money, enough everything.

Maybe they were right.

In 1990, when the International Mass Retailers' Association honored Sam Walton, founder of Wal-Mart, he insisted that the chairmen of Kmart and

Target come out of the audience and join him on the stage to share the spotlight. He told the audience that those competitors made his company work harder and were good for Wal-Mart and for the consumer. He shared his recognition with his fiercest competitors.

Sharing the stage is, unfortunately, a habit many people in business never develop. These are the people who:

- take the credit for other people's work
- try to make another individual or department look bad, assuming they'll look better by comparison
- are reluctant to tell a co-worker that his work is good for fear that this will diminish their own standing

> "Applause is the accelerator."
>
> —Milliken & Company

★ DON'T STEAL THE STAGE ★

Let's look at how an innocent but obnoxious action can steal the stage, jerking the recognition rug right out from under a proud performer:

A co-worker was admiring my just-completed first draft of this book on the day I had finished it when another co-worker came in. The first co-worker said to the arriving person, "Look—a whole book . . . already finished! Eight weeks. Can you believe it?"

The newcomer said, "Sure. My sister-in-law wrote a book in six weeks—longer than that one!"

What a letdown. I felt embarrassed that the first colleague was trying to give me a "famous" moment, but his show had been canceled by this insensitive thief.

That incident reminds me of the kind of person who, if you say you have a headache, says she has a brain tumor.

Resist the impulse to one-up, upstage, or change the focus during a co-worker's recognition moment.

KEEP YOUR MIND OPEN AND YOUR MOUTH CLOSED.

~ 10 ~
RECOGNITION ACROSS DEPARTMENT LINES

"Salespeople don't sell in a vacuum." That was the riveting lead sentence in publisher Bruce Matzner's recognition note to Terry Nicosia in a letter complimenting her for outstanding support as a manufacturing coordinator for *Drug Store News*. Terry handles production of the magazine, a business-to-business publication for the drug store trade. "The salespeople view you as an ally, not an adversary," wrote Bruce. "Your work with them has made the difference in closing some recent sales."

Wow. That letter traveled across a department line to make one woman named Terry feel valued. She kept the letter taped up on the entrance to her cubicle. Then she took it home and attached it with a magnet to her refrigerator door, where it remained for half a year. Friends, neighbors, and family read her memo and asked, "What's this all about?"

"So I'd get to explain it again to every person who came into my kitchen," Terry reminisced.

"That night," she said, "my husband, August, came home with a handful of pieces of paper. Each one contained words or sentences in eight different handwritings. He explained that he had been in a meeting at his job that day at the New Jersey Transit Authority. He and his teammates, all sitting around a table, were asked to write a comment about their impressions of each co-worker in the room. Then those 'secret ballots' were given to the person written about. I looked at his papers. 'Reliable,' I read. 'A true friend,' 'Great sense of humor,' 'His work is always done to completion and never has to be questioned.'

" 'Trustworthy,' 'A lot of fun,' his buddies wrote. He was so proud of those papers. I took my memo down to make room for his on the refrigerator door. What had always been display space for the children's drawings and school papers now had to make room for the proud adults in the family, too."

Terry and August were fortunate to receive written impressions from their co-workers.

Russell Justice at Eastman Chemical tells about recognition given across departmental lines across the world. The Kingsport, Tennessee, plant had been shipping boxes and drums of their chemical products to their plant in Singapore. A problem occurred in the Singapore warehouse. When employees went down the rows to look for the chemicals they needed, the labels from the containers had fallen to the floor, so they couldn't tell what was in them. Delays ensued, and customers were mad because they had to wait.

Labels weren't falling off at any of the other Eastman locations around the world, so one of the people in the Kingsport plant figured out that it must have been the 95 percent humidity in Singapore that was "unsticking" the labels. A new adhesive was found for labels bound for Singapore, and the problem was solved. The man in the Kingsport warehouse who had solved the problem received a note from Singapore thanking him for eliminating the frustrating problem that had been making their jobs difficult. Along with the note, he also received a Singapore flag on a little wooden stick.

Russell heard about this success story and went into the warehouse looking for the person who had solved the problem for Singapore. He didn't know the person's name or what he looked like. As he walked around in the warehouse, he saw a tow-motor coming toward him with the flag of Singapore attached to it, flapping in the breeze. He knew he had found his man. He stopped the driver, introduced himself, and asked him to tell him more about his solution. At the end of the story, the tow-motor driver reached into his pocket and pulled out a folded letter—the recognition note from Singapore. He had received the letter weeks earlier, but it still had a place in his pocket.

One of his buddies admired the flag and sent a telex to the person in Singapore, asking if someone might send along a flag for him as well. The telex came back. "No. We only give flags to people who help us."

"Well, how can I help you?" replied the man from Tennessee.

Too often the people we depend on for success are taken for granted. Or we only make noise when they don't get something done right or on time.

The truth is that very few of us can do our jobs successfully without help from people in other departments, cities, or even countries. Taking a few minutes to let them know we appreciate their help will make their day. Receiving recognition from outside one's own department isn't necessarily better than receiving from the inside. It's special in its own way, though, because outsiders don't have intimate knowledge of how we do our jobs; they usually see only the end results. Recognition from outside tells us that all our hard work is making a valuable showing out there in the world.

Cross the line.

FROM:	Rosas, Jessica
TO:	Sangster, Jimi (IS); Suarez, Julio (IS)
CC:	Smith, Darren (IS); 'janisallen@mindspring.com'
DATE:	Tuesday, December 01, 1998 5:00 PM
SUBJECT:	Thank you!

Jimi & Julio (Information Systems),

This is just a note to thank you for all your assistance in any and every question that I have ever presented to you. Your quick and courteous response when Wayne, Michael, Dan, and I call for help is much appreciated. Keep up the great work that you're doing and enjoy your holidays!

Jess:-)

TRY IT OUT!

Complete this flowchart of the people in your work process. It will help you identify people who earn your positive recognition:

My customers outside my department

_____
_____
_____
_____

Suppliers outside my department

_____
_____
_____
_____
_____
_____

Myself and my department

_____
_____
_____
_____
_____
_____
_____

My customers within my department

_____
_____
_____
_____
_____

Suppliers within my department

_____
_____
_____
_____
_____

My customers outside the organization

_____
_____
_____
_____
_____
_____

DEFINITIONS

- **SUPPLIERS:** People inside or outside your organization who provide you with material or information you need to do your job successfully.

- **CUSTOMERS**: People inside or outside your department and organization who depend on you for information and material.

> "When someone does a good job,
> applaud; it makes two people happy."
> —Samuel Goldwyn

~ 11 ~
# BOSSES ARE PEOPLE, TOO

The people who supervise us respond to positive recognition just like any other living being. In fact, you may be able to have a larger impact on your supervisor than on anyone else. Why? Well, supervisors tell me that they receive so little positive recognition, that when it comes, it stops them in their tracks.

Most supervisors care what their staff thinks about the way they manage. If you tell your boss that you appreciate the way she supported your ideas at yesterday's meeting, she'll know she's done at least one thing right that day. She'll not only feel good that you noticed, but she'll be impressed that you had the self-confidence to tell her.

Maybe you can see that your supervisor is under a lot of pressure lately and is working long hours to meet the department's performance goals. Just quietly tell him what you see that he's doing. It will make his night. The loneliest part of hard work and long hours is the feeling that "I'm the only one who knows what I'm going through right now." Recognition is just what the word says—seeing: recognizing what another person is doing and then telling him what you see.

Brad Chapman at Chevron Shipping—owners

and operators of oil tankers—sends daily recognition E-mails to his company's management team. "Not a day goes by," he says, "that at least one of them doesn't come by to tell me how much he or she appreciates it."

Don Ginder at Delta Faucet says, "You can influence your boss to change." His boss, Chuck, tells this story: "When I came here, Don didn't like some of my behaviors, and he told me he was going to help me change. He did!"

Don remembers, "Chuck was too involved (like a new boss should be) and the staff wasn't comfortable. The staff had meetings *without* our boss. One day I said to the group, 'He's going to be with us for a long time, so *we* need to change and help him change.' We made a plan that we would communicate with Chuck in two ways to influence him to be the boss we wanted:

"Each of us would tell him 'I liked this and that from yesterday's meeting.'

"And, if he had done something we didn't like, each of us would tell him: 'When you did so and so, this is how it made me feel.'

"One day, Chuck told me, 'This afternoon, five of you came in and told me you liked the same thing that I had done. I get the message.'

"Then he would thank us for thanking him, and we would thank him for thanking us. Today, we all say he is the greatest boss."

Can you use Delta Faucet's successful strategy with your boss? Think about it. What are some of the actions you appreciate from a supervisor?

Here are some of ours:

- gives me freedom to make and implement decisions
- takes time to look at my work
- gets help for me when I need it
- asks my opinion on how to handle a situation
- tells me about changes that will affect me
- asks occasionally about my family

- listens when I have a problem
- shows up in my work area with no agenda
- eats lunch with me occasionally
- teaches me new skills or arranges for me to learn
- includes me in meetings when decisions there will affect me
- talks positively about my work
- acknowledges when I'm under pressure or have a tough assignment

Those are actions that are easy to take for granted. But they all take time and extra effort. It would be easier for the boss just not to bother with many of them. When you notice your supervisor doing something you like, something that would be on your list, tell him. Knowing that you value it, he'll probably do it more often. And you'll get to watch the shock and surprise on his face when you tell him that his action is appreciated.

Here's a perfect example:

9/3/98

Deb,

Thank you for your time and patience to further explain details.

Also, thank you for your confidence in me.

I appreciate the special projects you have entrusted with me!

I look forward to new challenges!

—Cindy

TRY IT OUT!

Make a list of your boss's actions that help you succeed. Copy it and give it to him or her.

How my supervisor helped me succeed:

_____

_____

_____

_____

_____

_____

_____

_____

_____

SIGNED _____

Shock the boss with a little positive recognition.

~ 12 ~
TEAMWORK

What would team sports be without teammate recognition? Fellow team members are always the first on the scene to high-five the good pass, the block, or the point scored. They congratulate each other with smiles, pats, and hugs. Teammates are in "first position" to observe the exact behavior that has added value. On teams, there are five, nine, or eleven peers close by, greatly outnumbering the coach or manager.

The coach will get her chance to show approval for the successful play later, but she will usually be farther away from the action and the recognition will be delayed.

The world of work is a close parallel to team sports. Our team members are our co-workers. They're up close, in the know, and quicker on the scene than the supervisor. They also know how hard it is to do what we did. The power of recognition from a co-worker is the same as from teammates—receiving it reminds us that we're a valued member of the team.

At AFC Enterprises—operators of the Church's, Cinnabon, Seattle's Best Coffee, Popeye's, and Chesapeake Bagels restaurant chains—people nominate their co-workers for being "Team Players" as they see them working in ways that help others successfully serve customers.

Brad Chapman at Chevron Shipping participated in "boomerang" recognition—recognition that comes back to the sender—with people on his team. His department is part of a high-performance work team, that operates in an open-floor plan, with the number of team members

Have you high-fived a team member today?

BOOMERANG RECOGNITION

varying between eight and twenty, depending on the number of ships they are handling at the time. He and three of his co-workers sent management the following letter about Patty Villeggiante:

Patty exemplifies all that you would expect and more from an employee, whether it is ensuring that the fleet of ships receives exactly what they need when they need it at the best price, participating as a team member, or working on a special project. With Patty's never-ending support of everyone around her, she makes Chevron Shipping a better place to work. She improves the morale, attitude, and camaraderie of everyone she works with.
—Tom, Brad, John, and Geoff

Here's Patty's response:

. . . I was very touched and surprised. I can't tell you how much this means to me. I am still shaking and feeling so happy and proud inside. I care very much about the company and the people, and this made me feel that they care about me. Thanks again. I could just scream. Yeahhhhhhhhhhhhhhhhhhhhhhh!
—Patty

TIP: When you notice good work, mention it right away!

*Michael McCarthy

How to Give Recognition

VIII

~ 13 ~
"TELL ME ABOUT YOUR WORK"

The words above are some of the sweetest words in the English language. Most of us enjoy describing to an appreciative listener what we do for a living. It's always a surprise when the listener actually seems interested.

I'm much more likely to tell some people than others about my actions and accomplishments at work. Why do some people get on my "brag" list and others don't?

It's a result of their reactions when I've trusted them with my "proud time" in the past. I can think of two general categories: the person who stops what he is doing, focuses on me, and helps me feel valued and valuable; and the person who isn't sincerely interested in my answer, but wants to create the impression of giving me attention while actually thinking about something else.

What do those behaviors of these two opposites look like?

The effective listener and recognition-giver:

- Doesn't look rushed and actually enjoys listening for a few minutes.
- Asks about a specific aspect of my work in which he is genuinely interested.

- Looks at me while she talks and slows down her actions to take in the information and learn.
- Positions himself physically to avoid the inevitable distractions of passers-by.
- Makes *very* brief positive comments about what I tell him without taking the spotlight off me.
- Makes positive statements like "You must've felt great," or "That helped the customer."
- Resists the temptation to talk about other business problems or deadlines at that moment, and leaves me to savor the positive attention. He comes back or calls later to deal with the other subjects. He lets this positive experience stand alone.

The *faux* listener exhibits:

- Speed-nodding (the practice of bobbing one's head up and down at breakneck speed in an attempt to get the talker to talk faster or to wrap it up in a hurry).
- Interrupting to guess what happened next.
- Stealing the scene by jumping in with a similar experience that happened to him or someone he knows.
- Keyboard tapping and audible fidgeting when on the other end of the phone.
- Looking around "cocktail party-style" to see whom to talk to next.
- Finishing my sentences.
- One-upping—offering an idea on how I could have handled the situation even better, which kills any intended recognition.

As a listener, what happens if your sincere question gets you much more than you bargained for? We've all been that regretful questioner, when the answer was ten times more than we wanted to know about programming, land surveying, or whatever we asked about in the first place. If you have had this dreadful experience—in which you spent your time trying to figure out how to escape rather than learning the details of the talker's profession—you may understandably be reluctant to use listening as a way to give recognition to someone.

But listening while a person talks about her work is such a powerful recognizer that I believe it is worth the risk. Here are some ways to set the person up for success. These encourage him to give you enough information to make him feel good about his work, but not so much that you just can't listen to it all without screaming.

- "Jean, I'm on my way to a meeting in five minutes, but I'd love to hear how you managed to bring that project in ahead of schedule, if you have a minute to tell me."
- "Mike, I just heard about your presentation at yesterday's staff meeting. What specific thing do you think you did that caused them to buy your proposal?"

Brad Chapman of Chevron Shipping likes to approach people with, "I found your comment at the meeting insightful. Could you expand on it a bit for me?

"This gets you the double whammy," Brad points out. "It shows the person that you were listening to what he said at the time and that you value his further input now."

As you see, the questions above narrow the request for information to just what you want to hear. That works with some people, but not all. But it's worth a try, and you probably already know which of your co-workers will respond in kind. It's your chance to get onto someone's "brag" list.

Ask for what you want to hear, and then listen in celebration and without judgment or scene-stealing.

TRY IT OUT!

LUNCH & LISTEN

Make someone's day. Do a Lunch & Listen© with one co-worker. Tell him you would like to hear about his accomplishment over lunch. Eat a meal, and give him your undivided attention while he talks about something he's accomplished. Remember not to:

- interrupt to steal the spotlight and talk about something else
- tell him a better way he could have accomplished his mission

In the hour of talk time, give him fifty-five minutes. You take five!

—Feel free to make copies of the forms below—

LUNCH & LISTEN

To _____

I want to hear about how you _____

_____

_____

Let's have a Dutch lunch on _____ if you're free. I'd like to listen.

Signed _____

LUNCH & LISTEN

To _____

I want to hear about how you _____

_____

_____

Let's have a Dutch lunch on _____ if you're free. I'd like to listen.

Signed _____

~ 14 ~
THE IMPORTANCE OF IDEAS AND OPINIONS

Opinions are powerful instruments. Their volume gets turned up quickly, while discussions of facts and figures usually hover around normal decibel levels.

Most of us have worked and thought hard to develop what's in our heads, and we feel strongly about our ideas. Ever notice how even a person who's in a hurry will almost always stop to tell you directions when you're lost? Many of us feel we know the best way to get from here to there, the best landmarks to watch for, and an accurate estimate of how far it is. Often, we "overkill" by telling too much and confuse the poor, lost soul.

And keep in mind this is all given to complete strangers. Why this generosity of time and knowledge? It gives us a chance to help, but most of all, it gives us a chance to show off what we know.

A client of mine asked me to review with him some materials from a training class he had missed. Leafing through, I quickly breezed over a cartoon on one page in the notebook. My client reached across the table and turned back to the cartoon page as quickly as I had turned it over. "Exactly what do you want us to learn from this?" he asked, "I assume that everything you put in here has a reason, and I don't want to miss anything."

He made my day. I felt so smart that he had "backed up a page" to make sure he had the benefit of the smallest idea hiding somewhere in the recesses of my head. He valued my ideas.

Now a story closer to home: this book was written on my laptop computer. Usually, I draft chapters, print them out, and Michael edits and adds examples and new material to what he sees on the printed pages. I like to do it that way,

> "It's better to be looked over than to be overlooked."
>
> —Mae West

Letting go can be powerful recognition.

Let go.

Letting the other person have the "last word" can be powerful recognition.

because I can easily see the changes and additions he's made with his trusty weapon—the red editing pen. Then, sneaky as I am, I make the changes (most of them, anyway) on the computer.

I'm sure you're onto me by now. You can see that, by doing it this way, I have the last word. My ideas and opinions prevail.

Working on one chapter, I handed him the computer so that he could edit "real time," right on the screen. After a few moments, I couldn't stand it. I had to get behind him and look over his shoulder. I liked most of what he changed and added. But one deletion he made touched a nerve. I just had to keep that sentence in. So I tried to take the computer out of his lap. He saw me coming and held on. I tugged at the screen. He held onto the keyboard for dear life. We were both yelling for the other to stop.

Finally, we both relented when we were overcome with laughter at the ridiculous tug-of-war. Later, all I could think of was how we would have explained a dismantled computer to the people in the repair shop.

That tug-of-war was a struggle by each of us to have his ideas valued. It taught me one more time how powerful this feeling is. It is a valuable lesson. Respecting someone's ideas and opinions can also be powerful recognition. It taught me to recognize Michael for his contribution by cheerfully discussing his ideas and phrases, negotiating, and being willing to let go of my words. It works better that way, and he's more likely to spend time working on the book.

~ 15 ~
IF A TREE FALLS
AND NO ONE HEARS IT. . .

Sometimes it's better not to give attention to actions of co-workers. Unfortunately, those are often the times when it's the most tempting to pay attention. They are the times someone:

- wants to gossip more than just a little
- is complaining about something that no one can control
- is comparing herself to others—and the others are losing
- is wasting too much time when he should be doing something productive

If I join the person in those kinds of activities, I will give attention—which is the most powerful positive recognition known to man—and that will influence the person to continue, or even increase, his unproductive actions. I don't want to encourage this person because he's a distraction to me. But it's really hard to ignore him because it means withholding attention that he's "working" to receive.

And if I've historically been his audience to this kind of talk, he won't easily give up attempting to get my attention today.

The purpose of this chapter is to remind you that you are most likely providing positive recognition for whatever behaviors people are exhibiting around you. Most of us won't do something in a vacuum—for very long, anyway. It's back to that old adage, "If a tree falls in a forest, and no one hears it, did it make a noise?" If I want to cry "poor me," and no one lends a sympathetic ear, eventually I'll stop trying and crying.

I know what you're thinking. You don't want to be rude to your friends, so how can you stop paying attention to negative talk without damaging

ATTENTION is the most powerful recognition known to man.

your relationship with the person? It's risky. But we're talking about ignoring (removing attention from) the specific behavior that we don't want to encourage—that specific behavior only—not ignoring the whole person all the time. Here's what this looks like:

Godfrey Gossip comes to me and starts bad-mouthing another co-worker. He launches into a litany of everything that person is doing wrong. I react by immediately changing the subject without acknowledging the comments. For instance: "Hey Godfrey, I heard about that huge order you sent out yesterday. How'd you do it, man?"

Godfrey may be bewildered that you seem to be in a different conversation, yet talking to him, since you responded as if you didn't hear him. He'll say, "Did you hear what I just said?"

You: "Yeah, but I'd rather talk about that great order you moved outta here." If he persists, you can counter with: "I don't want to hear about that. It drags me down." Or, "Hey, man, let's talk about something else."

That works with some people, but there are no guarantees. Over time, though, most people respond to your consistent gift of attention—or lack of it. Just be certain you're giving attention only to the kind of talk you want more of, because whatever gets your attention will multiply and grow.

Give your attention only to behaviors you want more of.

~ 16 ~
PHRASING FOR PRAISING

In the early 1970s I worked with people in textile plants who were being encouraged to give positive recognition to each other. It wasn't easy for many of them. Looking a co-worker in the eye—maybe a hunting buddy—and saying, "You did good work" was just too uncomfortable to think about.

Somewhere along the way, the company began using items such as key chains, baseball caps, and pocket knives as an alternate way to let people know their work was valued, enabling supervisors to give a gift rather than speak words of recognition.

Oops. Though well-intended, that idea created problems instead of making recognition easier to give. People giving those trinkets often shoved them at folks, saying only "Here," as an explanation. People receiving them were left cold, as you might expect, wondering if management equated their valuable performance improvements with the cost of these two-dollar trinkets. We would have been much better served by giving words and attention, even if getting comfortable with this talk was difficult.

I believe it was difficult because many of us thought we had to give a flowery speech in order to give recognition. We might be able to say "I'm proud of you" to our small children, but never to another adult. We didn't have a practiced set of casual, brief expressions for letting someone know we saw their good work and appreciated it.

On my first job as a plant personnel manager, I interpreted my duties as being the mouthpiece of the company. Later, I was embarrassed to find out that my co-workers had nicknamed me "the walking policy manual." They couldn't see the real me under my protective policy shield and legalistic-sounding words.

Say it, but not with flowers.

Try not to sound the way I did. Avoid phrases like:

- "The department appreciates your efforts" (use "I" instead).
- "You are to be commended" (too passive).
- "That's acceptable" (gee, how exciting).

Dull, dull, dull!

Below are some words and phrases that work without overdoing it:

PHRASING FOR PRAISING

"That's a good idea"
"Nice going"
"That's a creative approach"
"Good for you"
"Wow"
"You didn't miss a thing"
"You've got the hang of it"
"First class"
"Way to go"
"That's really coming along"
"You make happy customers"
"You make me look like a hero"
"I really value what you did"
"You make our department look good"

"You've got the idea"
"Good catch"
"Glad you did that"
"I like the way you . . . "
"Excellent"
"Exactly right"
"Nice improvement"
"Cool beans"
"You did a ton of work"
"Looks great"
"I knew you could do it"
"That's the way"
"Good thinking"
"You get an A+"
"You made my day"

And resist the temptation to say, "Keep it up." Stop while you're applauding; don't ask for more work at this recognition moment.

PUTTING IT
INTO WORDS

TRY IT OUT!

What are your favorite "quickdraw" recognition phrases?

_____

_____

_____

_____

_____

FIRE ONE OFF RIGHT NOW!

~ 17 ~
POSITIVE GOSSIP

Talk about someone behind her back.

"Gossip" usually means saying something negative about someone. Why can't we talk about people behind their backs and make it positive?

Positive gossip is telling someone about something good another person has done—thorough research, careful planning, high productivity, or excellent serving of customers, for instance.

As your co-worker, I'm sometimes in a much better position to see your behind-the-scenes-work than our supervisor is, so I can let her know about your solid performance by relating some of these things.

POSITIVE GOSSIP

Alan, an IS Macintosh support technician, sent an E-mail to John, who supervises Efrain and Mike. Efrain and Mike had impressed Alan, as you will see, and he was quick to spread positive gossip to their boss:

"John, I just wanted to let you know how well Efrain and Mike performed last week with our office move. Not only did it go smoothly, but Efrain and Mike were extremely careful and patient with us.

"We had to move a large bench/workstation from the server room as well as make a total reconfiguration of our office. They took the time to make sure that sensitive equipment was not disturbed.

"Efrain stayed in constant communication to make sure that the office was set up so that we were comfortable and that we were 'down' for as little time as possible."

—Alan S. Plotkin

The icing on the cake will come when John later repeats those words back to Mike and Efrain. They'll get a double hit.

When people receive positive gossip, they have the satisfaction of knowing this good press about you has been in at least two people's heads.

Talk positively about a co-worker to a third person. It'll get back to her, and pack a wallop.

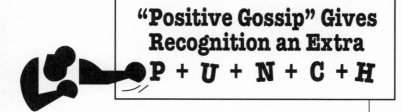

"Positive Gossip" Gives
Recognition an Extra
P + U + N + C + H

IX

Recognition Dos

~18~
PRE-PERFECTION RECOGNITION

If you've watched Richard Simmons's exercise video *Sweatin' to the Oldies*, it's immediately obvious that the folks doing the sweating are real people, not models or bodybuilders. Many look large beneath their sweatsuits and T-shirts, but all look happy.

After thirty minutes of aerobics to "It's My Party," "Great Balls of Fire," and "Dancing in the Street," Richard brings his thirty sweating students out one by one for a camera close-up during their cool-down.

Each person's name appears on the screen beneath his or her face, along with the number of pounds lost. After seeing six or eight names and "sixty-five pounds lost," "fifteen pounds lost," or "thirty-two pounds lost," one quite heavy woman dances toward the camera with a beautiful smile on her face. Below her name reads, "Just Beginning."

Watching this, I felt so proud and happy for that brave woman. I was delighted that she was willing to publicly take the first step toward her goal. It was something to celebrate. Most of us feel happy and proud of ourselves each time we do

The path to perfection is paved with small improvement steps.

something we've never attempted before, or make it to the first rung on the ladder of a personal goal. My hat's off to Richard Simmons for recognizing efforts and achievements at many levels, not just one or a few "winners" who had achieved the greatest weight loss or only people who now had perfect-looking bodies.

Speaking of winners, every one of those thirty people were recognized as winners. Simmons's recognition was given for improvement, not for beating the other twenty-nine. If he had recognized only the person who had lost the most weight, or met his or her ultimate goal, how many winners would we have seen? By applauding all improvements and actions—including "Just Beginning"—he was able to motivate many people in a way that would keep them (and us with imperfect bodies in videoland) interested, excited, and moving.

The secret of success lies in recognizing any improvement, no matter how small. Any contest or recognition method that stack-ranks, or compares people, or selects only the best one for recognition, fails. Even if it's for most improved, that still limits recognition to one person. It fails because it limits improvement by limiting recognition to only one person who improved, even though many might have improved.

When any co-worker makes that step in the right direction or makes something better than it was before, take ten seconds to recognize her efforts. Every good thing has a beginning. Be a part of that good beginning.

Anything that stack-ranks or compares people limits recognition and fails as a motivator.

~ 19 ~
THE SEXIEST MAN ALIVE

People magazine named fifty-eight-year-old Harrison Ford as "the sexiest man alive." His reaction was, "What is this thing they have for geezers? I've never felt sexy in my life."

Well, bah, humbug!

Obviously he either wasn't happy or wasn't comfortable with the cover story bulging from the racks of every grocery store check-out in America. Why would anyone have a negative reaction to such an honor? Most of us think we would find that enormously flattering.

Well, we don't know the inner thoughts of that humble actor, but I'll hazard a guess that if the magazine had written, "Harrison Ford made me believe that the invincible Indiana Jones had a deathly fear of snakes; I wriggled to escape the snake pit along with him," Ford would have enjoyed every word.

What's the difference? The "snakes" line was a specific comment about Ford's work, about his ability to convince an audience of a real quality of this character, and to evoke emotion.

Chances are it would have made the rugged actor break into his crooked smile and feel good. Naming exactly what someone did admirably will go a long way toward helping him to accept and soak up your compliment. This works because it's harder for the person on the receiving end to argue with the positive comments, and it only gives him that one specific compliment to live up to. I suppose that living up to "the sexiest man alive" is quite a tall order.

Here's a more down-to-earth example: I once told my manicurist after she'd finished my nails, "Nice job, Claudia. They look very pretty." Claudia's face wrinkled up. She looked irritated. "Well, did you think they wouldn't?" she snapped.

Let's rescue our "Indiana Joneses" from the "Temple of Gloom."

I didn't know what to say. I felt embarrassed that I had apparently insulted her. I felt hurt that she hadn't accepted my compliment about her work. Most of all, I just wished I could take back my words as if they had never been uttered.

Perhaps if I had told her, "That shape you give my nails is nice. They're just the length I like them," she would have accepted this very specific description more easily. Maybe she would have sat back and admired the shape herself and felt good.

Here's a description of the types of "recognition resisters" I've run into, and some ideas for how to communicate with them positively.

"RECOGNITION RESISTERS"

Type of Resister	Ways to Help This Resister Receive Recognition
"I'm skilled and experienced and you don't need to pat me on the back."	Use respectful methods like asking his opinions or including him in decisions.
"I'm embarrassed in front of all these people."	Give recognition quietly or send via E-mail or voice mail.
"I don't think I deserve it."	Make your positive comments as specific as you possibly can. Be low-key (don't exaggerate). Use "I" statements, such as: "Well, I saw the difference you made with that customer." Then let it go. She may never let you know she likes it.

~ 20 ~
DREAD RED NO MORE

We all get reports. We all have to read reports. And we all grew up dreading the sight of red marks on our school papers. A red circle meant "Something's missing." A red "X" meant "You guessed wrong, dummy." A question written in red demanded the completion of something.

But the red did get our attention. So now let's turn that attention to something positive. Instead of "dreading the red," let's help co-workers get used to looking for "recognition in red." Here's how:

- Keep a red pen handy.
- Draw a circle around a number on a weekly report that shows an improvement in someone's sales, reduction in errors, or improvement in quality. Write a short quip, like: "Ten percent better!" or "Way to go, Wayne!" next to your circle.
- Pencil in "I like this idea" in red in the margin of someone's memo.
- Sign or initial in red.
- Draw a red box around a well-written part of a report and sketch a face or something fun.

After your associates get over their surprise that red doesn't have to signal trouble, they'll start reading mail carefully, in hopes of seeing red.

DREAD RED NO MORE

TRY IT OUT!

THE TEST OF TIME

Perform a little time test. Look at the second hand on your watch while you read the following phrase:

"Steve, I'm glad to see you taking extra time to answer all of that customer's questions so patiently. You make our department look so professional."

Time elapsed? _____ seconds.

Value someone's work in the moment.

~ 21 ~
YOU HAVE A REPUTATION

When my stepdaughter, Shawn, was about ten, I noticed how good she was at noticing small things about people.

On a long Thanksgiving trip in the car, Michael was laughing at something funny she had said. He laughed and just kept laughing and couldn't seem to stop. Shawn and I started laughing at his laughing, and all three of us chuckled for a mile or two.

Later, Shawn said to me, "Did you ever notice how much fun Dad can have over a funny little thing? He can laugh at his own laughter. And the pitch of his laughing gets deeper, the longer he goes."

I was impressed with how finely she had discriminated even the pitch of his laugh, as well as her insight into why he kept laughing. I said, "Shawn, you're really good at noticing little things. That's a nice talent to have."

Months later, as she began to tell me about some small thing she had observed, she began by saying, "Janis, you know how you tell me that I'm good at noticing little things? Well, did you ever notice how Aunt Kayla always sounds so happy when I call to ask her if I can come over to see the cousins? She always gives me the same answer, in a happy voice, 'I'd just be tickled to death.' "

Shawn realized that she had a reputation for being a noticer of subtle behaviors and was eager to tell me some of the things she had noticed. I enjoyed hearing them and always said, "Shawn, you're good at noticing small things."

Seven years later, she plopped down beside me on the couch one day after school and said, "Janis, you know why I think Dr. Jordan is such a good Latin teacher? We can see her passion about what she teaches us. She starts talking about a story and she gets so into it. Her face lights up and she talks

Open your mouth and make someone famous.

"Use
positive
gossip to
spread this
person's
positive
reputation
around."

—Bill Lilly

faster. She uses a lot more gestures and talks loudly. She tells long, interesting stories. We students look at each other and smile, because we can see how much she's enjoying the stories herself. Seeing her passion kind of rubs off on us."

Even today, Shawn knows she still has her reputation for being a careful observer of people's behaviors, and I'll always be happy to recognize it for her.

Meanwhile, back at my client's office: My customer of nine years, John, was the last person to leave a meeting I had led. I had just checked my watch and adjourned the meeting by saying, "We've covered everything, and we're finished ten minutes early."

John stayed an extra minute and said privately to me in his quiet, professional way, "I'm not surprised. We always finish on time when you run the meetings." Such a small thing—finishing meetings on time. But there was a ton of positive recognition behind John's comment because he implied that he had been noticing it for a long time. Because he took a few seconds to tell me, I realized that this was a small behavior that he appreciated and that, in his eyes, I had a reputation for something, however small. It made me feel uniquely valued.

Most of us notice those small positive or unique things about the people around us. We just don't always take the time to tell them, or we don't think they care about our opinion. Wrong!

Think of some small habitual action that you appreciate in one of your co-workers. Tell him that you've noticed. Help him realize that he's famous for one specific action at work. Give him a reputation.

"I don't have a lot of time..."

~ 22 ~
TAKE MY MEETINGS ... PLEASE!

Many of us complain that we spend too much time in meetings. Too bad, we're stuck.

Let's use this meeting time—since we probably can't escape it—to recognize a co-worker who:

- offers a solution to a problem
- volunteers to take an action
- reports something productive she or someone else has done
- exhibits any positive behavior we'd like to see continued

Here are some "meeting methods" for recognition:

- Turn toward the person and say, "That's a good idea."
- If you're at a flip chart, write the name of the person next to the idea he just mentioned.
- Gesture toward the person to draw others' attention to something she's said or shown.
- Sidle up to the person privately after the meeting as you walk out. Tell him what you liked about his comment or report.

~ 23 ~
"I COULD TELL YOU, BUT THEN I'D HAVE TO KILL YOU" *

Brad Chapman of Chevron Shipping says, "People are sometimes so concerned about keeping recognition a secret until it's delivered that often they don't consider the feelings of the recipient. Who decided it should be a secret?

"We recently arranged for one of our Italian chief engineers to be flown to the San Francisco office. He was to be presented the President's Award at a meeting of almost forty people. He was being recognized for his development of a process to resurface cylinder liners in engines, which saved Chevron Shipping a huge amount of money.

"I noticed how surprised he looked when he was called up front to receive the award. After the event, he told me that his look had not been surprise. It had been two feelings. First, relief. Relief that he hadn't been called to the home office to be fired (usually the reason, he had observed).

"Next, he said, he felt terror. When he realized that he was expected to stand up and talk about his accomplishment, he was terrified of speaking in what perhaps he felt was not good English.

"Ouch! We had needlessly created a lot of anxiety by trying to keep recognition a secret."

Prepare people for public praise.

* From the movie *Top Gun*.

~ 24 ~
QUALITY RECOGNITION

When it comes to recognition, "quality" is defined by what the person on the receiving end wants. That person becomes your customer. Here are some tips on how to get customer satisfaction for the recognition you give:

- Give the recognition as soon as possible after you notice the correct behavior.
- Give recognition in private.
- Let the recognition stand alone—no add-ons of work or problem solving.
- Name the specific behavior or result you want to praise—no generalities.
- Give attention for the smallest discernible improvement, probably unnoticed by most other people in the universe.
- Give recognition at an unexpected time, not just in weekly meetings or at the end of a project.
- Start positive gossip to allow the person to hear your positive comments repeated by a third person.
- State the connection between someone's behavior and the group results.
- Specify how the person's performance added value to the organization.
- Use a specific comment as a lead-in to more general praise: "You got this done early. But I'm not surprised. You always do."
- Find out how the individual wants to be recognized and deliver your kudos accordingly (public or private, face-to-face, or via note, voice mail, or E-mail).

Go to the
trouble to
do it right.

~ 25 ~
RECEIVING RECOGNITION

Dig it if you deserve it.

Now put yourself in the role of the person on the receiving end. The more accepting you are of recognition, the easier you make it for people to give it to you.

Feeling humble or nondeserving sometimes prevents us from accepting positive comments. We may think that accepting means agreeing—agreeing that we did a good job. For some of us, that sounds too much like blowing one's own horn.

If this is how you feel, you can just say a quick and quiet "thank you." Or "It's nice of you to say that," if you want to share the spotlight. You aren't expected to give anything back when someone recognizes you, and you don't owe the giver anything.

David told his co-worker, "Christine, you designed a snazzy media kit." She replied, "Yes, I think it's pretty good." Christine gave the perfect response. It signaled that she, too, felt pleased with her work. Suppose she had launched into a litany of reasons why the media kit wasn't good enough or how it could have been better. That would've had the negative effect of correcting David, implying that he was wrong or didn't know a "snazzy media kit" when he saw one.

When I tell my mother she looks pretty, she usually answers, "I feel pretty." Perfect.

Don't kill the kudos!

Some people kill the kudos, though, and deflect the most sincere attempts to tell them that their achievement is valuable. Deflection—saying "It was nothing," or "It's just my job"—relieves our discomfort by getting us out of the spotlight fast. Michael calls these humble people "dastardly deflectors," evoking the image of a cartoon character hiding under a shiny black coat to avoid the contamination of a compliment.

Don't do this dastardly deed!

X

. . . And Don'ts

~ 26 ~
BACK-HANDED COMPLIMENTS
AND OTHER BLOOPERS

"You have a lot of energy . . . for a forty-year-old," I was once told by a participant in a training class. I burst out laughing as he gave me a confused look. It took him a minute to realize what he had said. His intention had been to compliment me, of course, but his qualifier showed both his youth and failure to realize how it would sound when his words floated out there. Pretty soon he was laughing with me.

Later I found a way to get back at him: "You have a good ability to laugh at your mistakes—for a person who makes so many." We laughed our way through the rest of the day.

That is one example of the bloopers that sometimes come out of our mouths when we attempt to give positive recognition to someone. It's not the only common one. We've got lots. And I'll bet you've seen some we've never heard of.

Recognition Bloopers and Blunders

Sure-fire ways to make someone feel bad instead of good:

 Saying something sarcastic after one person has given positive recognition to a co-worker.

In a meeting, a data entry clerk told us about how a co-worker had helped her catch up on her work when she returned from a two-day seminar. Her emphasis was on the work he did voluntarily. The man spoke up and told the group, "Yes, and she even brought me a cup of Starbucks this morning when she thanked me." Another person snarled, "Whose budget did that two dollars come from?" Talk about a party-pooper.

 Following the positive recognition with "but."

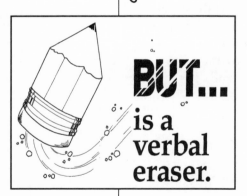

BUT...
is a
verbal
eraser.

- "Your report is complete, but it's five minutes late."
- "I see you rushed that order, but we'd better not have to pay rush charges."
- "These parts look great, but I don't think we can sell this many."

. . . We could go on, but we won't.

- Remember: "But" erases whatever good came before it.

Making a joke or disclaimer.

For instance, following the positive comment with, "I guess now you'll really have a swelled head, huh?"

Or this example, which, unfortunately, was done in front of millions of people:

A TV interviewer gave actor Anthony Hopkins a great compliment: "I think you elevate the work of every actor around you." Nice comment, until she added, "And I'm not sucking up when I say that. I have nothing to gain."

Blaaghhhhh. That spoiled everything.

👎 **Asking for more.**

An accountant noticed that the accounts receivable staff had increased their collections significantly. He wrote this E-mail to them:

"Congratulations on your 22 percent increase in collections last quarter. Of course, any further improvements this quarter will be welcome."

Oops. He had a good thing going with his first sentence. Then he blew it. Why? After reading his second sentence, it appears that his positive opening remark was just to soften the request for more collections—better known as buttering-up.

Perhaps he was sincere in appreciating the increase they had already worked hard for. If so, the best way to show it would be to let that recognition stand alone, without asking for more work or meeting higher goals. If he had given his positive comment and stopped, the accounts receivable staff could have savored the kudos for a few hours and likely would have pushed harder to beat last quarter's performance.

In an ad for Hallmark Shoebox greeting cards, a cartoon pictured the famous "little ol' lady" and her dog, Floyd. Floyd had been licking envelopes until his tongue was dry and sticky. The "little ol' lady" then tossed sheets of postage stamps onto the floor next to the dog and said, "Good job, Floyd. Now you can start licking the stamps."

To make your recognition work, resist the temptation to add new goals or requests for additional work in the same breath. If you need to talk about these things, do it later or do it beforehand. Just be sure the positive recognition stands alone.

> Recognition is applause time for what already is.

> "Now you can start licking the stamps."

~ 27 ~
RECOGNITION IS A
MANY-PERSONALIZED THING

I once had a big bucket of cold water figuratively thrown into my face while helping a colleague learn to conduct training classes. The person had been very nervous about getting up to present to a group, but he had the career goal of developing this skill for himself. He had carefully prepared to teach a one-hour segment during a seminar I was giving. He did a fine job. When he finished and the class members were taking a break, I said, "Tony, you made all the points clearly, didn't sound a bit nervous, and answered some very tough questions without getting flustered. That was good."

Tony looked at me and huffed. He then turned his head and walked out of the room.

Was it something I said? Apparently so. He didn't speak to me the rest of the day unless I spoke to him first.

At the end of the day over a glass of wine, I asked Tony what that had been about. He explained, "I'll never believe that I did a good job talking in front of a group, and I don't want to hear it. When you said it to my face, it made me angry. I wish I'd never gotten up there."

Whoa!

Well, that certainly helped me understand. Fortunately, it led to a longer conversation, which helped me learn even more. "When you send me E-mail notes or faxes, or leave voice mail messages to tell me that you like something about my work, I like it. I save them and re-read or re-play them. They mean a lot to me. I guess I'd just rather have my privacy when someone says something positive about me, and not have to worry about how to respond when I'm face-to-face with them."

That was one of the most valuable lessons I've

learned about personalizing positive recognition. If Tony and I had never had this talk, I'm sure that I would have continued to make the positive comments to him in person for a while. Finally I would have just stopped all attempts, feeling insulted with his spewing and stewing.

But the solution was simple: Give him positive recognition through some vehicle that allowed him to receive it privately, and *get out of his face.*

The biggest mistake some of us make in our attempts to give positive credit to co-workers is the same mistake we make when we buy gifts—we give people either what we would want to receive, or we give them what we think they should have, failing to even consider what that person really wants.

One Christmas I gave my mother her first automatic dishwasher. I had Sears install it, and I felt so happy that she would never have dishpan hands again. All the work it would save her, I thought.

Several months later she cooked a big Sunday dinner for the family. After dinner, my cousin and I ran her out of the kitchen while we cleaned up. We loaded the dishwasher to its fullest and turned it on. Then we went into the den to relax with her and my dad. The dishwasher quietly did its work. A few minutes later the little plastic cover containing the second dose of soap snapped open loudly, just as it was supposed to. The sound carried clearly into the den. Mother jumped up. "What's that?" She looked around anxiously. "Did somebody shoot a gun?"

Well, I guess this made it clear to everyone how often Mother had been using this wonderful gift I had given her. When I gave her the third degree about it, she admitted that it hadn't been turned on since the installer tested it months earlier. "I'd just rather wash my own dishes," she apologized.

No apology needed. I should have apologized for carving out that valuable block of cabinet space,

This stuff ain't easy, but what is?

which took away some good storage. I hadn't bothered to find out if this was a gift she wanted. I only knew that it was something I liked, and something that I wanted her to have. Fifteen years later, the dishwasher still sits there unused taking up space, reminding me that I did more harm than good by not personalizing my gift—not finding out what she really wanted.

If we find out how our co-workers would like to be recognized, we can avoid all this waste. When we've worked with a person for a long time, we've usually had opportunities to watch their reactions in many situations. We can usually predict whether they would like face-to-face recognition or whether they're like Tony and would prefer a private note or E-mail.

When we don't know the person well enough to get it right the first time, it's fine to try one method and see if it works. If it doesn't, it provides an opportunity to talk (as Tony and I did) and find out what kind of recognition they really like.

~ 28 ~
OR BETTER, STILL . . .

Eavesdropping on two women dining at a neigh-boring table in a restaurant, I heard one ask the other, "Have you seen your grandchildren lately?"

"No!" the grandmother snapped. "I've decided that those grandchildren should see their grand-mother being treated with some respect or not see me at all!"

There's definitely a story there. Reading between the lines, I'm guessing that it is not about a lack of respect, but about a grandmother who has tried to improve upon her son's or daughter's par-enting skills and been told to back off. Grandmotherly advice can be wonderful if it's asked for, and sometimes people ask for help and they really do want it.

Anyone with more experience almost certainly has better methods to do everything, from feeding babies to preventive maintenance of machines. But sometimes discretion truly is the better form of valor.

I'm the world's guiltiest of knowing the best way to get something done and, unfortunately for the people around me, foisting my favorite methods on them. The first time my husband and I entertained together, he asked what he could do to help prepare the food. Delighted with his offer, I asked him to arrange cheese and crackers on a plate. When he proudly showed me his finished work of art, I remarked, "Don't put broken crack-ers on the plate. Put those back in the box. You can't serve broken crackers to our guests." He had clearly committed hospitality heresy, and I lost no time correcting him.

How excited do you think he was to entertain after that unpleasant experience? Not very. In fact, I couldn't figure out why he became reluctant to invite people over. Duh.

Don't let broken crackers break relationships.

The title of this chapter is a very dangerous phrase. It's an excellent and efficient way to punish someone's idea or accomplishment. Most of us find our own positive recognition in solving problems, so when a co-worker tells us about a solution she just used, our brain cells line up to calculate a better or faster solution. We love a challenge, but we love even more the feeling of meeting the challenge—offering a better way.

I'm too quick to give advice. And I sometimes focus more on my excitement about my truly wonderful idea than on the real needs of the person I'm talking to. Maybe I can change . . . if I learn to bite my tongue.

As "Dear Abby," advises, "The most unwelcome advice in the world is that which is unasked for."

XI

Building Improvements to Higher and Higher Levels

~ 29 ~
YOU GO, GIRL

Dawdling in the housewares aisle at Wal-Mart, I noticed two sales associates conferring: the older woman, Joann, nodding, while the younger woman, Michelle, wrote something on the inside of a shoebox lid. "Perfect," said Joann. "Now tell them your name somewhere in there."

"I just don't know if I can do it when I get to the microphone," Michelle admitted. "Well, just read it right here and now to me, for practice," Joann encouraged.

Michelle quietly lowered her eyes to the cardboard script, reading slowly but clearly. Joann gave her full attention, nodding and smiling. When it was finished, Joann said, "Just like that. Don't change a thing. Go!"

The young associate practically ran to the front of the store. Within a minute I heard, "Good morning, shoppers, and welcome to Wal-Mart. Today in the shoe department we have lots of new styles we've just put on the shelves—cool shoes you won't want to miss. My name is Michelle. I'll be looking for you. Thank you."

Michelle put down the microphone, breathed a sigh of relief, and hurried toward her department.

She put on the brakes and a big smile when she saw Joann standing in the aisle with her arms outstretched for her. It was a wonderful day for them both.

Time elapsed: start to finish, six minutes.

What can we learn from this success story? Will Michelle do this again? Let's name some of Joann's actions that helped set up Michelle to succeed:

a. She looked attentively at what Michelle had created.
b. She added ideas without criticizing what was already done.
c. She suggested that Michelle practice and gave herself as an audience, creating a safe opportunity to build confidence.
d. She made positive comments about Michelle's practice run.
e. She suggested the next step: "Go," meaning do it quickly.
f. She showed up at the site of Michelle's performance and celebrated her success immediately.

Set someone up for success with "help-full" words.

Items *a*, *d*, and *f* fall into a special category. They're the correct response after the fact when a co-worker has done something you want to recognize. All the other actions set Michelle up to succeed: *b*, *c*, and *e* were "help-full" suggestions; *a*, *d*, and *f* acknowledged her success afterward. That is positive recognition, and it increases the probability that the person will continue to do this action again and again.

The crucial difference between "help-full" suggestions and "or better still" comments is this:

- "Help-full" suggestions are given *before* someone begins a job.
- "Help-full" suggestions *add* to someone's chances for success.
- "Or better still" comments are given *after* a job is done.
- "Or better still" comments *take away* from someone's feeling of success.

Let's look at some additional ways to help co-workers succeed. The real key lies in positive and helpful words, versus critical words. It's easy to see the difference in the following list:

CRITICAL WORDS	"HELP-FULL" WORDS
"That's not right . . ."	"Try this . . ."
"No, no, no . . ."	"Next time, use . . ."
"I have a problem with . . ."	"Handle it this way . . ."

Are you offering help...or criticism?

As Marcos, an associate art director, told me about his supervisor, Mary Jo, "She never looks at my design and says 'That stinks.' She always says, 'Here's a different way to do it.' "

And Maria, an administrative assistant, gets help in succeeding from Pam, who asks Maria key questions pertaining to the project at hand.

"This pushes me in the direction I'm comfortable with," Maria said, "while interjecting Pam's bright and creative ideas to help me."

Also, looking back at the Wal-Mart story, we can make an educated guess why Joann was the co-worker whom Michelle went to for help. Michelle had obviously had enough experiences with Joann to feel safe. She knew she wouldn't be criticized, and that she would come away feeling better, not worse.

The most important insight here is this: There may have been other Wal-Mart associates in the store that day who had much more experience writing and giving speeches, and who would have changed Michelle's first draft unrecognizably with the best choice of words imaginable. Maybe Joann herself could have thought of some better words or some better ideas for the speech or suggested a smoother way of delivering it.

But the wisdom in Joann's method was in the confidence it gave Michelle that her ideas were

She affirmed the direction her co-worker was <u>already</u> heading, and then <u>got</u> <u>out</u> <u>of</u> the way.

worth keeping, and that she was ready for her first big step. Joann's behavior allowed Michelle to perform the task, and then quickly feel the fulfillment and pride that comes when we struggle at something and complete it to our satisfaction. That's called *earning* our recognition.

That approach builds self-confidence and works easiest in small steps. What Joann saw was a golden opportunity for Michelle to take her first step at once. She affirmed the direction Michelle was already heading and then got out of the way.

This happened to be a situation in which it was not critical to be perfect. If those co-workers were two people working in a chemical plant, where actions must be precise in order to be safe, we wouldn't want to see such quick encouragement of a merely acceptable behavior. Where lives can be threatened or customers poorly served, it's necessary to make sure people meet exacting standards to avoid serious mistakes or damage.

You can judge the kind of situations where it's safe to encourage co-workers to proceed as opposed to criticizing any detail that isn't perfect. Just realize that we don't have to have perfection the *first* time. It's not always necessary to correct, change, or criticize another person's work or idea.

Whenever you see an opportunity to help someone take a step, perform, and gain some self-confidence (without threatening the business or people's safety), remember some ideas for communicating, phrases like these that demonstrate your confidence in the performer:

- "I know you can handle this."
- "You decide."
- "I know you can do it."
- "Use your judgment."
- "Your experience will guide you on this."

SETTING OTHERS UP FOR SUCCESS:

Can you think of someone who has helped you succeed during your career?

*Who?*_____

Write him a note, or tell her what she did to help you.

Select a co-worker who could use some help to succeed right now.

*Whom did you select?*_____

How can you set him up to succeed with "help-full" suggestions and give him positive recognition for small steps or small improvements?

*"Help-full" suggestions:*_____
_____
_____

Positive recognition comments: _____
_____
_____

SETTING UP OTHERS TO SUCCEED

~ 30 ~
MISTAKES OR SUCCESS TRIALS?

Thomas Edison's familiar explanation of inventing the light bulb ("First," he said, "I discovered 9,999 ways not to make a light bulb.") teaches us that working toward a goal is paved with many mistakes and dead ends.

There are three productive ways to respond to "failed" attempts and mistakes:

i. Document the process that produced the mistake, then change that process (process improvement).
ii. Brainstorm productive uses for the "mistake" (the Post-It solution).
iii. Celebrate the "success trials" on your way to your final product (the Edison/Allen method).

The first method, process improvement, involves creating a flow chart of the process and then determining which part of the process is creating the error. Correcting the process will correct the end product of the process. The third method, celebrating success trials, is a good way to encourage yourself and your co-workers to persevere in your efforts to overcome problems.

THE POST-IT SOLUTION

Post-Its were invented by a 3M chemical engineer who was working with adhesive formulation. It was a failure, because the adhesive failed the tests of adhesive strength.

A member of his church's choir, the engineer needed something to mark his place in his hymnbook, but which could also be moved and wouldn't damage the pages of the hymnal. He applied this "failed" adhesive to small notepaper, and the rest is history.

Woody Allen (a distant relative, no doubt) once said, "Eighty percent of success is showing up." He was speaking as an actor and comic who had to show up at auditions to get work, enduring rejection after rejection. After so many, the temptation is to read about another advertised audition and think, "Why bother? I'll probably be rejected again. I'll just stay home."

Thomas Edison knew the "showing up" secret when he assembled a team of researchers to create an electric light bulb. He and his team tested more than ten thousand substances in his workshop in Menlo Park, New Jersey, before they found one that worked. It took many months. When the team was discouraged by yet another failure, Edison would say, "You've just discovered another way not to make a light bulb. Keep it up."

Thomas Edison was recognizing the attempt because he knew that the failed attempts were the path they must take to reach success. As Edison himself said:

"Genius is only 1 percent inspiration and 99 percent perspiration."

Sometimes in training classes when I've asked participants to work on difficult paper assignments, I invite them to rip the draft page out of their binder, crumple it noisily into a ball, and throw it ceremoniously onto the floor in the middle of the classroom.

We then name those crumpled balls "success trials" instead of mistakes. We count their number and laugh at them and make it okay to throw away our first attempts to succeed. That relieves all the pressure to do the task perfectly the first time.

People sometimes cheer when another paper wad lands on the floor. The shock of pitching trash on the floor and the relief of laughing gives us a totally new way to look at the learning process. We go on to create new documents and feel proud of the pile of paper balls, which helped us get to the final draft and to success. No one feels like a failure.

If you never try to succeed, you'll succeed at never trying.

One time a member of the hotel cleaning staff came in while we were at lunch and cleaned up the mess. When the class members returned and discovered the paper balls missing, they became upset and started raiding trashcans up and down the halls, desperately dumpster diving, trying to reclaim their precious paper wads.

Celebrate your steps of progress and, before you know it, you'll arrive at your goal. If you wait for perfection, you may never get to celebrate. When one of your co-workers makes a mistake, say, "That was one attempt," "You got a result," or "I see a success trial."

TRY IT OUT!

EDISON/ALLEN SUCCESS TRIAL METHOD

Jot down an attempted solution that didn't work. I'll bet you learned something from the experience. Re-frame it in your mind as a success trial, and if it will make you feel better, copy this page, wad it up into a ball, and throw it onto the floor. And be proud of it!

MY SUCCESS TRIAL	MY SUCCESS TRIAL
1. Something I've done in the last twelve months that wasn't right the first time: _____ _____ _____ _____ _____ *Signed* _____ 2. Wad paper. 3. Gleefully toss.	1. Something I've done in the last twelve months that wasn't right the first time: _____ _____ _____ _____ _____ *Signed* _____ 2. Wad paper. 3. Gleefully toss.

- You can claim Certified Professional Success Trial status when you have kept three success trial paper wads on display in your cubicle.
- Advance to Elite status when you have explained those to a colleague without embarrassment.

XII

Obstacles

~ 31 ~
REAL MEN DON'T GIVE RECOGNITION?

When former pro wrestler, Navy SEAL, and Vietnam Veteran Jesse "the Body" Ventura won the race for Governor of Minnesota in 1998, his friend Arnold Schwarzenegger sent him a large bouquet of congratulatory flowers. When Jesse saw all the roses, he said, "Did I die?"

Since when do men send flowers to each other? All this warm and fuzzy recognition talk and pats on the back may sound like New Age sensitive guy stuff. Frankly, that's the response I heard from some people in the early '70s.

My guess is that these reluctant recognition givers were hesitant because they feared the reaction they would get from the person on the receiving end.

Not only do tough guys have to worry about being seen as sissy, but women also worry about whether we're coming across as businesslike and assertive enough. It's a miracle that anyone ever has the self-confidence to break down and tell a co-worker they're proud of her work.

Alex, a manager in the office copiers business, told me about his first-ever attempt to give positive recognition to his assistant. He realized he'd been taking Lisa's good work and her initiative for granted, so he walked out of his office and into her cubicle one morning carrying a report she'd written.

"Lisa," he began, "I just want you to know that I've always noticed your initiative to separate the numbers by region from each week's production report and send it out so people can see their performance right away. I've never told you this before, but it helps all of us when you do this without my asking you to do it."

Lisa's face was frozen as she stared up at Alex, who was standing by her desk. Finally, she broke her silence to say, "Why did you really come out here, Alex?"

Poor Alex didn't know what to say, so he stood with his mouth gaping for a moment. "That was all," he finally mumbled and went back into his office.

Sitting there, he said, he realized that must have been the first time in four years of working with Lisa that he'd ever told her he appreciated her work. He could hardly blame her for being skeptical about his intent. Her question implied that she assumed Alex was buttering her up prior to asking for something.

So, yes, we do take a risk of getting a put-down when we offer recognition. Sometimes it's because people don't trust our motive when they've never heard recognition from us before. Sometimes it comes from their own feelings of not deserving recognition, or embarrassment at not knowing exactly how to respond when they hear it.

After Lisa reads this book, she'll know how to keep Alex's recognition coming. All she has to do is say, "Well, thanks," or smile. Any positive response from her is likely to make Alex want to make positive comments about her work again. Just as powerfully, any negative words, sarcasm, or rebuttals from Lisa will probably send him into recognition retreat.

We don't need to analyze ourselves or our co-

Don't send your co-workers into recognition retreat.

workers, or look for someone to blame. The solutions are to increase the frequency, specificity, immediacy, and personalization of the recognition we give, as follows:

- Give recognition often enough to allow giver and receiver to get used to it.
- Say only what we mean, and say why we like their action (sincerity).
- Name the exact action or performance we want to recognize, avoiding suspicious generalizations (specificity).
- Give the recognition quickly after we notice it (immediacy).
- Discover a meaningful, non-embarrassing method of giving recognition to each individual (personalization).

SSIP HUNT

Making recognition specific, sincere, immediate, and personalized are the keys to success. Those increase the chances that the receiver will receive it well. On the following page is a recognition memo sent from one co-worker to another. Go on a treasure hunt for words and phrases that demonstrate:

- Specificity
- Sincerity
- Immediacy
- Personalization

Then circle them. See how many SSIP treasures you can dig up (I excavated twenty-two). Use those techniques when you write your recognition notes (and for more information on SSIP, see *Performance Management* by Dr. Aubrey C. Daniels).

Circle the specific treasures that make this letter effective recognition.

TO: Bernadette Casey
FROM: J. Roger Friedman
DATE: November 15, 1996
SUBJECT: Headlines

Dear Bernadette:

I have been impressed with the headlines in the last few issues of *Drug Store News*. They read well and gave a sense of urgency. The November 18th issue is an example of what I am referring to—I liked the headline on page 1 and on page 3. The verb "stunned" and the adjective "murky" are excellent choices of words.

Congratulations.

Sincerely,

J. Roger Friedman

JRF/hl

cc: Fred Filer
Marie Griffin
Bruce Matzner
Sandy Sutton

~ 32 ~
"GIVE RECOGNITION? NO TIME!"

Most people are busier at work than they were a few years ago. Each of us is doing the job that more people used to do. Customer demands for quick answers, instant changes, and just-in-time deliveries mean that everything moves faster. When would anyone have time to take on extras, like going around telling people what a good job they're doing?

So, let's concentrate on positive recognition that can be given "on the run," or praise that can be delivered in the normal course of doing our jobs, with half-a-minute's pause.

Meaningful moments can be made for co-workers without taking the time to write a note, stage a party, gather people around, and without spending a dime. Below are some ideas for giving quick recognition on the spot, with nary a word uttered:

- smile
- nod
- keep quiet and focus all your attention on the person
- give a "thumbs up"
- give two extra seconds of eye contact after hearing a comment you like

Want some "quickdraw" ideas?

- While having coffee or lunch with a buddy, say "You know what I like about how you do your job?" Then tell exactly what you've noticed. What a great feeling he'll get!
- While on your way through a work area, try to notice what someone has done well. Take five seconds to tell her: "Hey, that chart's looking good!"
- When you spot a co-worker doing the correct method for a job, tell the person.

"You can see a lot by observing."

—Yogi Berra

Name it and walk.

- When you see someone taking the trouble to perform a task safely, such as bending his knees to lift a box, say, "I see that good knee-bend," and keep walking. Two seconds. Name it and walk.
- Give lots of small, quick comments during the day. Don't wait for perfection. Don't make a big deal out of it or wait until someone holds a special recognition event.

XIII

Self-motivation

~ 33 ~
LET'S MAKE A DEAL

I've used deal-making to write this book. I enjoyed writing it, but it was very easy to work on other things that I could have quickly checked off my to-do list, or fulfilled a project with a tighter deadline. So I resorted to deal-making with *me*. Each time I completed a chapter, I allowed myself to check my E-mail. Since reading my mail is something I enjoy, I used this little bargaining to get my book written.

Maybe you prefer making phone calls, walking to another department to check something with a co-worker, or working with your favorite software as your reward. Whatever it is, you can choose a favorite work activity, which you have freedom to do at your discretion, and give it to yourself as a present for completing a perpetually procrastinated task. You can do this five or ten times a day!

Also, you can make a deal with a co-worker to set your respective goals and a joint reward. On a day that looks like it might be tough to get all your work completed, find a close associate who's in the same boat. Break the workday into two or three parts, with a goal for a percentage of work completed for each two- or four-hour block for each of you.

Let's make a deal.

At ten A.M., for instance, agree to go for a walk outside for five or ten minutes if you have both finished what you wanted to complete. If you work in an office, going out together for lunch might be your reward for reaching your noontime goal.

A sub-goal could be to have lunch in together if you both complete 75 percent. Use the lunch time to brag about what you accomplished, if you feel like it. Or talk about anything but work if that would refresh you more.

For instance, you and a trusted co-worker can agree to become "success partners." Here's how:

Prepare a list of potential "deal" rewards to arrange for each other when you meet your goals for the day's work.

Each of you keeps your success partner's list in a file, and pulls it out to help celebrate her accomplishment.

SUCCESS PARTNER IDEAS

For_____

Given to_____ on_____

Methods for helping me celebrate my accomplishments:

_____   _____

_____   _____

_____   _____

Thanks for being interested in my success.

—You may copy this form—

Below are some thought-starters for simple, quick, easy ways to deliver rewards:

- Sit still or stand still for a few minutes in a quiet place and just watch what's going on around you. It's called taking a break.
- Tell a trusted co-worker what you're proud of about the work you've completed—or the work he's completed.
- Eat candy from the vending machine with no guilt.
- Stand back and look at the work product you've just created, if it's tangible. Or think about it, if it's intangible.
- Savor the task, thinking about how it's done uniquely or well because it's *you* who did it.
- Tell your success partner what you're thinking.
- Call someone you enjoy and talk for three minutes.
- Take ten minutes to spend with the person you always wish you had time to talk to.

A Spoonful of Sugar

Helps the Medicine Go Down

TRY IT OUT!

LET'S MAKE A DEAL

List your work activities in reverse order of how much you enjoy them:

1. _____ (least favorite)

2. _____ (so-so)

3. _____ (neutral)

4. _____ (not too bad)

5. _____ (more favorite)

6. _____ (most favorite)

Go down the list, completing each task, using your favorite as your reward.

Or, make a one-for-one bargain:

When I complete _____ ,

I'll allow myself to_____ .

—You are welcome to make copies of this page—

PROUD TIME

~ 34 ~
ASK AND YOU SHALL RECEIVE: FISHING FOR COMPLIMENTS

I once had a boss who wanted to give me positive recognition for the projects I worked on, but he traveled most of the time and just wasn't there to see and know what I was doing. Receiving recognition from him was important to me, so I decided to give him some help. When he came into the office, I'd give him a minute or two to get his coffee and settle down, and then I'd appear in his doorway and declare, "Aubrey, you might miss an opportunity to recognize me if I don't tell you about this."

"Well, you'd better tell me about it right now," he'd smile. So I'd tell my story, and he'd listen and say positive things. It was a little joke between us, but one of amusement, not insincerity. I could signal him in order to set him up for success as the giver of positive recognition.

Some people might not be comfortable doing this, either on the giving or the receiving end.

Showing off isn't showing off if it's true.

They might think this "asking-for" approach would devalue whatever recognition it elicits, so those folks won't choose this method of getting recognized. But I know I appreciate it when co-workers let me know about successes they've had—events or results I would have had no way of knowing if they hadn't told me.

On the receiving end, I'll take all types of positive recognition. There are enough sources of frustration and negative feelings around; I choose to invite positives and to allow them to soak in when they come. Or, as we say in Sandy Mush, where I grew up, "Just *waller* in it."

In our family, Michael and Shawn and I ask each other for recognition when we've accomplished something that makes us proud. After I mow the lawn, I'll sometimes ask Shawn or Mike to "come out and give me some proud time." Freshly cut grass looks much better when additional eyes look at it, I find.

When Michael builds a new set of shelves or makes some other improvement in the basement, he urges us downstairs to admire his handiwork. Shawn and I always stop whatever we're doing when he says the magic words, "I want some proud time." We know he needs only thirty seconds or so, and we remember how good it feels when he stops his work to give us proud time. After "That looks really good, Dad" and "It's great to have that extra storage, Michael," he's satisfied and goes back to work. We return to whatever we were doing. It's a positive moment for the family, and it refuels the person who has done the work.

It's okay to ask a trusted co-worker or supervisor for a moment of her time to look at what you've created. But we've all had the experience of showing a piece of work to someone who immediately tells us how they would have done it differently, or how we ought to change it. This is the person who believes it is his role to improve on everything he sees and to bring his knowledge out and show it off at every opportunity. So don't ask him for proud time.

Again, the qualifier here is "trusted co-worker." Trust in this situation means that he will affirm my work *if* he likes what he sees. He will honor my request for proud time. That is why it's important to preface the showing off of your work with a sentence that tells the person that you wish to show off. "I want some proud time" or "Would you help me celebrate the completion of this project?" are some ways to signal what you expect and want. It's like inviting someone to a party for yourself. A simple statement will set the other person up to give positive attention to what you've done and not look for problems or give advice.

If you know that your work isn't finished, let the person know that ahead of time. Tell her that you're 50 percent complete or that you're showing her your first draft. It's a signal that you simply want a pause to refresh yourself with a friend; you want acknowledgment of progress, not corrections and edits.

As a Hollywood director used to say to his guests after showing them his new film: "Tell me how you loved my movie."

"No brag, just fact."

—Walter Brennan,
The Real McCoys

FISHING FOR COMPLIMENTS

"She's just fishing for compliments."

This disparaging remark is made about anyone who seems to be "showing off" or calling attention to his accomplishments. Such a person is thought to be either insecure or an egomaniac. In our society we take a dim view of either.

▼

Positive reinforcement is the fuel for behavior, like oxygen is the fuel for fire.

When someone is "fishing for compliments," she is simply seeking fuel for her behavior. In electric generating plants, air is force-fed by blowers into the combustion chambers to fuel the flames to optimum efficiency. The output is the energy that moves our society. No one questions the wisdom of feeding oxygen to boilers, or accuses the engineers of "fishing for oxygen." This is because we see the value of the output: electricity.

This is the paradigm we have to break: that "fishing for compliments" is bad. Certainly, a constant demand for attention can get to be too much in its extreme, but when we get requests to look at someone's work, we can ask, "What is the person fishing for?" If it's approval of a behavior or a result that we want that person to repeat, then the attention, the compliment, is worth our time to give it. We wouldn't want to force-feed oxygen to a burning building; similarly, we want to be sure we are complimenting only productive behaviors—behaviors that achieve worthy ends.

The new paradigm is:

▼

With compliments for bait, achievement will be the catch of the day.

My friend's ten-year-old daughter was unusually helpful to him one night in helping to cook dinner, clear the table, and load the dishwasher. He told her how helpful she was, and gave her a big hug. She disappeared upstairs, he thought to spend the remaining time until her bedtime with her Nintendo game. Soon she called, "Dad, would you come up here?"

On the erasable "white board" mounted on his office door was her just-created rating scale, designed like the customer feedback cards she's seen on tables in restaurants.

> Dear Dad,
> Please tell me how you liked my help with dinner. Was I
>
> ___ Unhelpful   Any Compliments?
> ___ Helpful   _____
> ___ Nice   _____
>
> Love,
> Shawn

After completing his rating for her and giving her a smile and another hug, he wondered about her use of the word "compliments." Was she mistaking it for the word "comments," commonly seen on restaurant rating cards? Maybe. Maybe not. No matter. She used it to get what she wanted . . . compliments. And she got them.

Reprinted from the June/July 1991 issue of *Thumbs Up* newsletter.

~ 35 ~
RECOGNITION AT A TABLE FOR ONE

"To Dad from Dad," the label on the package under the Christmas tree happily announced, in Michael's familiar handwriting. This was the year that he realized he could give presents to himself.

Self-recognition is like giving presents to ourselves. No, it *is* giving presents to ourselves. Self-recognition, when you get down to its mechanics, is:

- allowing ourselves to be proud of what we've accomplished
- making time to savor the good feelings

My goal with this book was to write one hundred pages. The night the page counter at the bottom of my computer screen rolled over to those beautiful triple digits, I was sitting at a gate in the Tampa airport. I quickly saved my work, shut down the computer, and looked for a stranger I could accost with my good news.

Everyone looked exhausted and indifferent, so I raced, computer case swinging from my shoulder, to the airport's Burger King. I greedily treated myself to a large order of hot, crisp, salty fries and a "bucket" of Diet Coke.

I wanted to mark my happy occasion, celebrate the achievement of my hard-earned goal, and eat French fries guilt-free for once in my life. Are you turning to page one hundred now to check for greasy fingerprints?

Anyone who posts a positive note he's received on his cubicle, bulletin board, or—like Terry Nicosia—refrigerator, is using self-recognition. Whether anyone else ever sees it, we know it's there.

Anytime you stand back for a moment and admire your work, you're giving yourself positive recognition.

112

Stand back and admire your work.

Anytime you re-live an accomplishment in the car on your way home from work, you're recognizing yourself.

Anytime you put your good work in a "keep forever" file and then go back and look at it, you are practicing self-serving recognition.

Anytime you allow yourself to feel satisfied enough with your work to take a break and savor it while you walk or eat or drink or smoke, you're dishing out kudos to yourself.

Few of us would want to live on self-recognition alone because we also know our work is valuable when other people tell us. But self-recognition is an excellent and available source. And we can be sure it won't contain criticisms—unless we're perfectionist self-critics. It can supplement the positive words we get from others. It can serve us a snack until our companions arrive for the next recognition repast.

Be self-serving.

XIV

Relationships and Your Team

~ 36 ~
CRITICISM

Sir Isaac Newton is said to have been so sensitive to criticism that he withheld the publication of a paper on optics for fifteen years until his main critic was dead. Dead! Most of us can't wait that long to let our work be seen.

We've all seen co-workers clam up and stifle their good ideas when a negative person is in the room. Our history with certain individuals teaches us that some people will find fault with almost any suggestion or solution that's mentioned. Over time we delete them from the invitation-only audience to our ideas. "New ideas are fragile and all too easily killed by criticism," observes Daniel Goleman in his book, *Working with Emotional Intelligence*.

"Well, this is just constructive criticism . . ." we've all been warned. There's no such animal. If your sincere intent is to help someone improve, refer back to page 89 of this book and reread Mary Jo Scibetta's masterful phraseology. (Okay, so you don't want to turn back. I'll spoil you. She told Marcos, "Here's another way to do this," when she could've said, "That stinks.")

We can redirect people's actions by telling them what to do next time, since "Last time," as my

"Last time is just a memory."

friend Jay says, "is just a memory."

Another way to improve on an idea without killing it with criticism is this:

Suppose a co-worker proposes a process change in your customer service that will eliminate some unnecessary steps and make response time shorter, but will require costly new software. Knowing that, most of us automatically would offer: "You're crazy. We'll never get the money for that software."

DOWN WITH IDEACIDE

Here's a way to stop yourself from committing *ideacide* before giving it time to breathe and possibly live a long and profitable life:

Say, "Betty, that software would improve our response time, and I'd like to find a way to demonstrate enough savings to pay for it, say, in the first year."

That comment is an engraved invitation to work with the idea and make it workable, or at least to keep it breathing long enough to find out if it's viable. In addition, it avoids punishing the person who offered it, and if it doesn't work out after some research, the idea person will feel satisfied, not insulted.

Time doesn't allow for such care to be taken over every idea that's mentioned. But this is a choice you can make if:

- the idea has merit and if the obstacles can be overcome
- you'd like to hear more ideas from this usually quiet person

"Don't find fault, find a remedy."

—Henry Ford

The above technique is what I call "idea-building," and it works in meetings or one-on-one. It has two parts:

Name what you like ("Betty, that software would improve our response time . . . ").

Ask for ways to make it work (" . . . and I'd like to find a way to demonstrate enough savings to pay for it in the first year").

Down with ideacide!

TRY IT OUT!

IDEA-BUILDING

Use idea-building when:

- the idea might be a good one, but would create other problems if implemented
- the idea is almost, but not quite, workable
- you need commitment of the whole group

How to idea-build:

Say something specific about why this idea is good:

"I like this idea because _____ ."

Make a request to overcome the problem with this idea:

"and I'd like to find a way to prevent _____ ."

Those two parts must be expressed together, and in the order shown above.

~ 37 ~
FEELINGS

Sometimes the workplace gets emotionally charged and feelings flare up. But generally, once those feelings have been expressed, they either dissipate or can be put into the background while the work moves on.

I've learned a lot about reacting to other people's feelings in recent years. The most important thing to know about feelings is that you can't change someone else's. Trying to talk someone out of his anger usually makes him angrier. Telling a co-worker "You shouldn't feel that way" is a ridiculous waste of your breath. "Shouldn't" and "feel" don't fit together in the same sentence. Think about it. If a friend said to you, "I'm tired," you wouldn't answer, "No, you're not." That would be pretty goofy. Only that person can speak about his or her own feelings.

The best way to respond when someone says, "I'm swamped!" is to say, "I see you have a ton of work," or respond in any way that acknowledges the feeling she has just expressed. It's not necessary to agree with her or even offer sympathy. And here's the most important part: You don't have to solve her problem. That includes not offering solutions, like "Well, if you'd learn to use this new software, you wouldn't have that problem."

Don't try to talk her out of her feelings. For instance, "Be glad it's not worse," or "You should be happy to have a job" is not what she needs to hear while she's feeling downtrodden and overwhelmed. The important thing to remember is that whatever the person is feeling probably is not a permanent condition, and it may have changed by the next time you see her. Sometimes it relieves some of a person's pressure just to be able to verbalize what he is feeling. And that's all he needs at the moment.

"Shouldn't" and "feel" don't fit together in the same sentence.

My biggest error when people express negative feelings to me is to try to fix the problem for them, or at least offer advice on how they can fix it. I have to keep reminding myself that if a person wants advice, he will say, "Janis, I need your advice." If he said, "I'm offended that no one asked me before they made this change," a careful reading of his sentence tells us that he is *not* asking for advice; he's making a statement about how he feels. So stifle the advice. A good response would be, "I can understand your reaction." This is not agreement, nor is it necessarily sympathy. It's an acknowledgment—just a message sent: "I hear you, and I'm not going to try to talk you out of this feeling."

Let people have their feelings.

Ironically, trying to talk a person out of his feelings usually makes most people cling more tightly. If we feel that we aren't being heard, we will come back with further explanations, convinced that we didn't make ourselves clear the first time. We still have the need to prove we feel the way we feel.

Allowing the person to feel "heard" can often free him up to move on quickly to more productive topics. And when you think about it, it makes my job as the listener easier, too. I don't have to be responsible for offering or implementing the right solution or for going to bat for him to solve the problem. When I've acknowledged his feelings, I've done my job.

When a person is tired, under deadline pressure, feeling ignored, or angry, it's *his job* to have feelings that reflect what's going on in his world. And it's *my job* to hear him and let him know he has been heard. It's surprising how easily most of us can let go of whatever has snagged us as soon as we feel heard. Feeling heard by one other human being suddenly makes us feel less alone in our pain or frustration. It's the loneliness that compounds the feelings—the fear that no one else understands. So don't play psychologist. Don't listen eternally. Don't agree. Just hear and let him know you got his message.

Let him know he has been heard.

DRIVE OUT FEAR

One of quality expert W. Edwards Deming's 14 points is "Drive out fear from the workplace."

Is there fear in your workplace?

Driving out fear can't be done overnight, but you can do it gradually by doing a few things consistently:

1. *Change what you do in meetings. When results have been disappointing, give your time and attention to people when they suggest ways to meet goals in the future. DON'T spend time asking "Why wasn't this done?" or deciding whom to blame.*

2. *When one of your associates tries one of her own ideas, tell her you like the initiative, even if it didn't work.*

3. *When you see one of your associates using an approach to solving a problem that is different from the way you would do it, watch and wait, and try to keep your mind open and your mouth closed. His different approach might work, you might learn something, and your associate will "learn" not to be afraid to use his own ideas, even if they're different from yours.*

Over time, actions like these will drive out the fear by driving in trust, patience, and respect.

Keep your mind open and
your mouth closed.

TRY IT OUT!

LET PEOPLE HAVE THEIR FEELINGS

For practice, jot down a few phrases you would feel comfortable using to signal that you've heard a co-worker's expression of feelings, without:

- sympathizing
- solving
- separating him from his feelings

Here are a couple. Add a couple in your words.

- "Gosh. That's a pain, all right . . . "
- "I see your point."
- "Wow. That is frustrating."

_____

_____

_____

_____

_____

_____

_____

~ 38 ~
I'M SORRY

Yogi Berra didn't speak to George Steinbrenner for fourteen years after Steinbrenner had one of his staff tell manager Berra that he was fired from the New York Yankees team. Steinbrenner didn't break the bad news himself. Berra vowed never to set foot in Yankee Stadium as long as Steinbrenner owned the team.

But in January of 1999, Steinbrenner made a trip to the Yogi Berra Museum in Little Falls, New Jersey, took the former Hall of Fame catcher by the hand, looked him in the eye and said: "I know I made a mistake by not letting you go personally. It's the worst mistake I ever made in baseball."

Berra accepted his apology and replied, "I made a lot of mistakes in baseball, too." Then he gave Steinbrenner a tour of his museum, and said he would consider returning to Yankee Stadium next season.

Steinbrenner got it right. He came to Yogi Berra's turf, looked him in the eye, admitted he had been wrong, and stopped there. He didn't explain why he hadn't fired Berra himself, try to tell Berra that he shouldn't hold a fourteen-year grudge any longer, or defend his actions. With no strings attached, Yogi could accept his apology. "It's over," declared Berra (who, as you probably remember, famously said, "It ain't over till it's over").

I'm sorry.

Those two little words are two of the most important words in relationships with other people. Sometimes, they're the most difficult to say. But they're often the perfect solution to a disagreement, angry words, or an insensitive action.

I find that bruised feelings are often the underlying cause when a co-worker suddenly starts giving me the cold shoulder. I sense it when he starts

"I'm sorry"— two of the most important words in successful relationships.

speaking to me in a clipped and businesslike manner, avoids eye contact, or fails to tell me about things he would normally be quick to inform me about.

Usually, I can think back to an event that caused the change of behavior toward me, but not always. The first step toward mending the relationship is to check out my guess of what caused the coolness. Not with an encounter group, a sensitivity session, or hocus-pocus, but with a quietly, privately-asked question such as: "You seem a bit distant, and I wonder if I was insensitive in not including you in the project planning meeting last week?"

Sometimes the person will confirm that this was indeed the cause of his feelings, if it's true. Sometimes he won't admit it even if I have guessed correctly. He may say, "Oh, no, I didn't want to be involved in that, anyway."

If that is his response, you may say something like, "Well, I was just thinking I might have made a mistake by not asking you to help us," and leave it at that.

If that was the cause of the problem, the acknowledgment on your part is likely to be enough to help the person let go of his hurt and move on.

Acknowledgment of responsibility (for offending or slighting someone) and apology are powerful medicine for relationship-healing.

Acknowledgment and apology will often cure what ails us.

If you didn't guess correctly what caused the problem, the olive branch you've extended may serve as a first step toward melting the ice. It may not, but you've lost nothing except a minute of your time. We don't recommend prolonging a discussion about "what's wrong" by playing a guessing game for twenty minutes or pleading with the person to tell you. A scene like that can end up giving the pouting person more attention and "in-the-spotlight" time—which means recognition—for acting cold rather than for becoming receptive to your attempts to re-create a healthy working relationship.

So, if the person wants to pout for a while longer and isn't ready to smoke the peace pipe, just give it some time. Some people in this world get their jollies from feeling like a victim and will fight you all the way to cling to their misery. If you work with a person like that, and she has not responded to your honest, nonblaming attempt to acknowledge and apologize, just accept that you can't make her change, and put your energy somewhere else.

Be polite to her and keep her informed of business information relevant to her, but let her sulk, if that's what makes her happy. You can't patch up the relationship all by yourself. It takes two to tango.

Speaking of the tango, the dance floor is where I learned a valuable and funny lesson about apologizing. When Michael and I took lessons in ballroom dance, Alexander, our Belorussian instructor, told me in his delightful accent, "Now, when the gentleman steps on the lady's foot, the lady always says, 'I'm sorry.' Why? Because it's always her fault for putting her foot underneath his."

Alexander gave me a wide, expectant smile, hoping I would see the humor in his advice. I did.

Soon Michael's foot landed on top of mine, and I switched my grimace to a grin, saying as sweetly as I could manage without laughing, "I'm sorry!" Michael smiled, appreciating that I was willing to play Alexander's game to let him off the hook blamelessly.

With this small and seemingly insignificant experience, I learned how a smile and an apology, and not caring whose fault it is, can work wonders. It created smiles all around and added a bit of tongue-in-cheek to the cheek-to-cheek.

My dentist has earned the nickname "the sorry dentist." That is a compliment. Here's why. Each time he sees me flinch under his probing and poking in my mouth, he says, "I'm sorry." I know that he didn't do it on purpose, and I expect to be hurt, at least a little, when I go to the dentist.

I'm just impressed that he's so quick to acknowledge my momentary discomfort and express apologies. I immediately react with the thought "it wasn't that bad." Somehow the fact that he notices and names my pain gives me the feeling that I'm not all alone. When he says, "I'm sorry," I switch my focus from me to him. I want somehow to signal to him the assurance that I'm okay, and that he's doing a good job. Then the two of us become partners in our goal of minimizing my pain.

That may sound like a heavy interpretation of a simple situation, but I think of it often when I'm dealing with more serious and longer-lasting problems.

Remembering my "sorry dentist" nudges me to be quick to offer an "I'm sorry" to someone who's hurting, even if I did nothing—or did nothing intentionally—to hurt them. Judging by the facial expressions I usually see, it sometimes helps.

If love means never having to say I'm sorry, maturity means being willing to say I'm sorry.

Notice and name someone's feelings. It helps them feel that someone is sharing their burden, and it's less lonely out there.

Shawn once said to me, "You hurt my feelings." By doing that, she taught Michael and me the perfect way to express hurt. Then one of us could apologize or ask questions to learn more. It's such a simple thing, but adults forget that we can say that, too. Shawn tells us that she was taught to say it in pre-school, when she was four. A valuable

"I'm sorry." Say it to yourself ten times and get comfortable with it.

Maturity is being willing to say "I'm sorry."

lesson for us "sophisticated" adults.

"You hurt my feelings" is a phrase few of us would be comfortable saying to co-workers. It's too bad, because hurt feelings are precisely what's at the root of many problems. Perhaps we can find a way to communicate our feelings honestly without feeling like a vulnerable child. For instance:

- "I felt excluded."
- "I felt awkward."
- "I felt taken for granted."

The nice thing about "I" statements like those is that they do not accuse the person we're talking to of wrongdoing or ask him to change his behavior. They are less likely to precipitate an argument. Who can argue with "how I feel?"

Some of our co-workers will respond to statements like that by stopping to consider their actions, and maybe even apologize. Some of them.

Apology Accepted

In order to be effective, an apology is just like recognition. It must stand alone. No extra messages can be tacked on. For instance, don't justify your actions during an apology (or maybe ever).

"I'm sorry I criticized you in front of the whole department meeting, but I just didn't want us to go off on a wasteful tangent." Does that really sound like an apology? No. It sounds like I'm still saying the same thing I said when I offended the person. That sentence will probably make it worse.

Don't try to teach the person a lesson.

"I didn't mean to embarrass you, I just want you to get it right the next time." Playing wise parent is out of place during an apology.

Apologies are such strong statements, they can stand just fine on their own. It takes a ton of self-confidence and courage to say, "I'm sorry." Don't undo it with a terrible trailer. Say it and stifle.

The right moment to apologize is just a few

An apology is not an apology if you're still explaining.

seconds before you feel ready. That may sound like bad advice, but I say it for those people like me who would never be 100 percent ready to apologize, just hanging onto that thread called "But I was right!" So I need this little ticking clock to tip me over the edge and get it said. Then I'm always glad I did, because it softens the other person immediately, and we can get on our way to much more fun times.

Apology: Say it and stifle.

~ 39 ~
WHO CARES WHO'S TO BLAME?

If we don't care who's to blame, we can increase innovative solutions to problems big and small.

The real secret to creativity of all kinds is quantity. Produce many attempts (quantity) and you may inevitably yield the creative break-through (quality).

This idea runs counter to the traditional wisdom that says that the creative process can't be switched on like some mass-production machine. Artists are heard to say, "I have a creative block. I'm waiting for inspiration."

But when we read the biographies of famous artists, we find that quantity was the key to their productivity. Michelangelo made five thousand sketches in preparation for painting the Sistine Chapel ceiling. He didn't wait for inspiration to strike. He warmed up his inspiration muscles with sketching exercises. In other words, he worked until the inspiration hit.

Imagine what would have happened if Michelangelo had been criticized for early less-than-perfect outcomes. "Not good enough, Michelangelo," grunts the critic, looking through his sketches and frowning. "If you can't come out of this slump, we'll have to send you back to school and get some new talent, like that kid, Raphael."

If you criticize your co-workers for their honest mistakes or for failing to produce the particular result you're looking for the very first time, then you short-circuit the improvement process and kill their motivation to experiment and take risks.

Instead of searching for someone to blame for mistakes or less-than-perfect attempts, look for

"A man would do nothing if he waited until he could do it so well that no one could find fault."

—John Henry Newman

ways to prevent recurrence. When two people are engaged in work and a problem or mistake comes to light, there are two choices we can make in where to cast our gaze:

1. We can look at the other person and point a finger.
2. We can look at the problem and pinpoint the cause and solution.

When we choose option number two, we have freed up all of our energy to focus on the problem, with none wasted on casting blame. This option creates healthy, positive relationships and allows us to move more quickly to find a solution for the problem.

Make the problem our enemy, not each other.

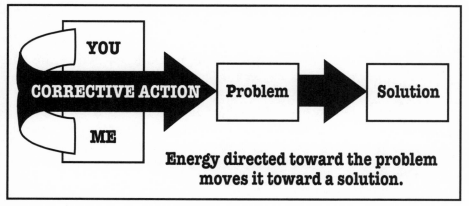

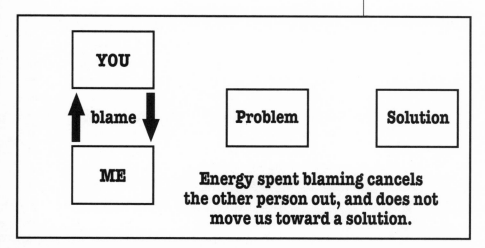

~ 40 ~
BE JEALOUS,
OR EARN YOUR OWN RECOGNITION

W.W. told me that he left his last job as a body shop foreman after eight years because of the parts supervisor. One Friday, he said, the shop manager was out and asked Fred, the parts supervisor, to hand out all the paychecks. When Fred walked over to give W.W. his check, he whistled and smirked, "Boy, I didn't know you made this kind of money, W.W. Maybe I better get a job on the shop floor so I'll be rich, too."

W.W. forgot about Fred's comment at the time, but the next day Fred paged him and told him to go to the parts supplier and pick up a special-ordered bumper needed today. W.W. went immediately. The warehouse clerk could not find the order. W.W. insisted that the clerk search her orders and ask the other clerks if they knew about it. W.W. called Fred, who insisted that the order had been placed the day before, and that a crew was now waiting for it.

Everyone searched again, but no bumper and no order was to be found. Finally, W.W. returned to tell Fred the bad news. Fred had gathered two other people around and was laughing as W.W. walked in the door. "There was no such order, W.W. I just thought anybody who makes that much money ought to stay busy all the time, so I was just giving you something to do."

Unfunny jokes like that continued until W.W. decided to quit. Now working elsewhere, he has worked his way up to the job of shop general manager in two years. It's too bad for his previous employer that jealousy prompted such negative actions. We've all seen people treat co-workers this way. It doesn't always result in someone's leaving the company, but it gets in the way of positive working relationships and co-operation.

Jealousy:

—Wanting what someone else has.

—Assuming the only way to get it is to take it from him.

There are two root causes of jealousy:

- wanting what someone else has
- assuming that the only way to get it is to take it away from him

We want a piece of the pie and assume that the amount of pie in the world is fixed. There is nothing wrong with wanting something. The problem is with the second assumption. As Bill Lilly at Ocean Spray says, "The theory of abundance teaches us that success breeds success, and there's enough for us all."

There is always more pie in the world, but you have to bake it. There is always more recognition in the world, but you have to earn it. If Fred, the parts supervisor, wants more money, he can learn how to earn more. W.W. made his money the old fashioned way: He earned it.

When someone receives some recognition that you'd like to have, ask how they earned it. Then do the same thing yourself and make sure the right people know about it. This won't always work, but it works often enough to make it worth your while. You don't catch fish every time you go fishing, but you'll catch some often enough to make fishing worthwhile.

Just remember what Jimmy Buffett says: "If you caught fish every time you cast, it would be called 'catching.'"

You can bake your pie and eat it too.

TURN PROBLEMS INTO SOLUTIONS

Marsha, the mother of a fifteen-year-old daughter, uses positive phrasing to create a win/win situation for them both. When Meagan wants to go visit her girlfriend and Mom wants Meagan's room cleaned, she says, "You may feel free to go over to Sarah's as soon as you have cleaned your bedroom."

That sure beats, "No, you can't go, because your bedroom is a mess." Mom gets a clean room, and Meagan gets fun at her friend's.

~ 41 ~
SHOWING RESPECT FOR CO-WORKERS

Among the best ways to show respect for our colleagues is to ask for and listen to their opinions and experience.

Listening sends a message to the person talking. The message can include:

- I'm interested in what you're saying.
- I want to learn from your experience.
- I defer to your knowledge in this subject.
- I respect your opinion.

Of course, it shows good manners on the part of the listener when she maintains silence while the other person finishes, and looks at the talker even when distractions are present.

I'm not the best listener in the world, but I try to work at it in every area of my life. I only answer my ringing phone when no one else is with me. My office is in my home, so sometimes this means I'm with a business associate; sometimes I'm with family members. Voicemail dutifully takes a message. I believe whomever I'm talking with at the time is more important than an unknown caller.

Answering the phone just because it's ringing is a hard habit to break because I was brought up to drop everything—and everybody—when the phone rang. But with messaging devices everywhere, we can always call someone back whose call is important to us. In this way, we can give uninterrupted, undivided attention to all.

Silence is a golden gift we can give again and again.

Listening is one of the most powerful ways to show respect and also to give positive recognition. It's an "in-the-now" method. We always have ears with us, the only tools we need to give this kind of respect and recognition.

$hhhhh !

> ## The right word may be effective, but no word was ever as effective as a rightly timed pause.
>
> —Mark Twain

~ 42 ~
ENTITLEMENTS

Once upon a time a company decided to give small recognition gift certificates for several "above expectations" performance areas. One area was perfect attendance. No one was expected to have perfect attendance all the time, but for those who did come to work every day, the company wanted to give some recognition. No one lost anything if he didn't have perfect attendance; this was purely a bonus for those who could and did come in every day. Apart from the other performance areas, it only amounted to a few dollars added to the gift certificate.

After the first gift certificates were awarded, some people complained loudly that they missed the perfect attendance portion because they had been sick and "it wasn't fair." Some people said, "You're knocking us out of our gift certificate. What do you want us to do, come to work sick?"

The people in charge of the program quickly decided it was more trouble than it was worth.

Recognition is always an "extra" given through the free will of the other person. We are not entitled to it, nor is it owed to us. We are entitled to our paycheck only when we've worked.

When a teammate angrily asks, "Why didn't you notice that I finished my work early?" the idea of recognition isn't fun anymore. It's work.

Offer recognition generously. Accept recognition graciously. Nobody owes it to you.

Gracefully accept the recognition you do receive, and graciously give recognition to the efforts of others. Don't expect it or demand it. That kills the fun for you and others. Any recognition given to you under duress of demand may not be altogether sincere—which shouldn't come as any surprise. You end up feeling resentful about what you didn't receive instead of feeling good about the recognition you did get.

Michael's dad, John McCarthy, had a company car for many years that he could drive home in case he was called to a job site after business hours. At some point, the IRS ruled that companies must calculate the value of vehicles and require employees to pay taxes on this value. His company decided to discontinue the practice of allowing the cars to be driven home.

Michael remembers saying, "It stinks that they've taken away your car after all these years." His dad replied, "I'm not angry about this. It has been a nice bonus that I had for all these years. We were never entitled to it."

"This reaction put it all into perspective for me," Michael said. "The car was not something of ours that was being taken away, but rather something given as a bonus benefit year by year. That we had had the car, was something to feel good about, not something to feel bitter about when it was no longer available.

"Thanks, Dad, for teaching me this valuable lesson."

XV

Families and Personal Relationships

~ 43 ~
FAMILIES

As you already know, all of these ideas about recognition and relationships aren't just limited to people at work. The principles work the same with all people. And family members are people, too, even if sometimes we don't act like it (toward each other). In ballerina Gelsey Kirkland's autobiography, *Dancing on My Grave*, she tells about her first performance that her father ever attended. After the performance, her mother told her that her father had left the auditorium abruptly before the house lights came up. He had been in tears. Apparently, though, he couldn't let his daughter see that he approved of her dancing.

Gelsey wrote: "When I returned home, I found my father alone in the dining room. Neither of us said a word. After an awkward silence, I blurted out, 'Well, was that good enough for you?' " He didn't answer, and she rushed from the room. "Not only was our love blind," she wrote "it was mute. A paralysis of the heart rendered us incapable of an exchange as gracious and as simple as a compliment."

When Gelsey was a student at the New York City Ballet, Madame Doubrovska, a teacher, said to

Families need recognition too!

her: "Oh, Gelsey, you were marvelous yesterday, technically wonderful; but, you know something, dear, you didn't make me cry."

From these stories, it seems that Gelsey had more than her share of messages as a young girl that she could never be good enough to please the important people in her life. The rest of the book goes on to tell of Gelsey's unhappy adulthood and her problems with relationships, with drugs, and ultimately, a suicide attempt.

Successful writer Susan Sontag said in a 1992 interview in *The New York Times* that she never felt smart. "Wasn't your mother proud of you?" the interviewer asked. "My mother was a very with-holding woman. I would put my report card by her bed at night and find it signed at the breakfast table in the morning. She never said a word." Such stories make us want to shake the parents to get some positive words out of them. We know they feel proud of their children. Why can't they tell them? We'll never know all the reasons, but what we can take from those sad events is the determination not to let it happen in our own families.

Some parents are reluctant to give their children positive recognition because they are afraid the child will think "Okay, that's good enough. I can stop trying now," and become complacent and lazy. So the parents ("for the good of the child") keep raising the bar and wait until the child has accomplished 100 percent to say that they are pleased. Perhaps they're waiting until the child successfully completes grade school. Then high school. Then college. Then gets a good job. Then has a family. Then becomes a good parent. Then what?

This may be a natural act for parents in some ways because most parents see their roles as always helping the child to the next step in life. And that is an important role. But it can send a negative and fearful message to the child if he is never given praise for what he has done so far.

"She never said a word."

In her book *Behavior Analysis for Lasting Change*, Dr. Beth Sulzer-Azaroff describes a technique she has developed called positive scanning. Positive scanning will direct our attention to the behaviors we like (positive behaviors) to such an extent that we begin to not notice the negative ones.

We can use positive scanning at work and at home. Focusing on the positive behaviors helps us learn to ignore—not to see—the unpleasant ones. Here's how it works:

A married couple saw that their relationship was eroding after many years together. Their daily life seemed to be dominated by complaining and bickering. Neither the husband nor the wife wanted to end the marriage, but they needed help. Dr. Sulzer-Azaroff coached the couple literally to begin counting their mates' behaviors that they liked. "He makes coffee and sometimes breakfast, doesn't he?" asked Dr. S.

"Yes, but why should I count that as a positive? He's always done that," said the wife.

"Is that nice for you, or would you rather do it yourself?"

"Oh, no. It's just fine the way it is," answered the wife (notice her reluctance to say anything positive).

Dr. S. said, "So count this. Then find two more positive things today."

After several days and coaching sessions, the wife had listed three of her husband's positive actions she had "scanned" each day. Dr. S. encouraged her to scan for four the next day.

"Forget it. I'll never find four," she said. "Can't I list the bad things too? That only seems fair."

"No way," Dr. S. replied. "Our job is to scan for the positive actions. Seeing them will cause you to focus on them. If you mention them to your husband, he will increase their frequency. This is how it works."

After finding four positive behaviors per day for several weeks, the wife decided to raise her

> Scan for positives. Recognize them. They'll multiply.

goal to five, and in another week, to six.

Then the husband got involved, and his experience was similar to his wife's. Pretty soon they were both up to nine and ten per day on a regular basis.

Notice that no one was raising the goal for the husband or the wife to do more positive behaviors. The total focus was on what both could note and count during their scanning. This sounds backward because it all began because the husband and wife wanted behavior changes in *each other*.

The solution came because they were willing to make behavior changes in *themselves*—a change to notice, count, and mention the positive actions, rather than noticing and mentioning the negative ones. By focusing on each other's positive behaviors, they both produced more of them. Their relationship became happier.

Every day we do helpful things for others, and others do helpful things for us. Some of these we take for granted because it becomes routine and expected. Don't limit your positive scanning to new behaviors or heroic events. If you can notice a behavior that you would miss if it disappeared, recognize it to your loved one. Scan for positives. Say something positive about them. They'll multiply.

Here's a great example:

Marcos, an art director, reports: "Sometimes my wife says to me, 'Alexander is very lucky to have you for a father.' What a feeling!" Looks like Marcos' wife is a positive scanner.

POSITIVE SCANNING
Feed the Right Behaviors and They'll Multiply

~ 44 ~
EVERYTHING I NEED TO KNOW
I LEARNED FROM MY STEPDAUGHTER

Shawn is very wise for her seventeen years. She has a way of communicating her wishes:

- that places no blame if something isn't as it should be
- that puts focus on the future, not the past
- that forgives
- that relinquishes "talk time" to others

And all these she communicates with scant few words.

When her dad gave her a verbal phone message "Noelle wants you to call her" and produced no phone number, Shawn didn't complain that he hadn't written Noelle's number down. Instead, she said, "Next time, Dad, would you please write down the person's number for me?" He smiled and agreed, mostly influenced by Shawn's chosen, cheerful way of making her request.

When we became a family, Shawn was ten. She looked up at me at the dinner table one night and said, "Just for future reference, I really like tea with no ice in it." What a pleasant way to ask for what she wanted, rather than say, "I don't like ice in my tea." Usually, she serves herself, but I always remember that pleasant request when I'm pouring.

"You couldn't help it," she comforted, when I dropped her favorite cereal bowl, and it shattered on the terra cotta kitchen floor. She sent me the "I'm not upset" signal before I had a chance to react. No crying over spilt milk around her.

"No, you go ahead" is her consistent invitation when she and I begin a sentence at the same time. Which makes me want to hurry up and finish my sentence so I can return the floor to her. It's refreshing to listen to someone who wants to listen to me first.

It's refreshing to listen to someone who wants to listen to me first.

Those are all personal skills that make communication and relationships flow smoothly and softly. Wish I could say she got them from me!

. . . *the piano teacher said, when his student missed a note. "Oops" is a nonjudgmental way to get someone to stop and "re-do" an action. "Oops" conveys that you know the other person made a mistake without intent and allows the performer to put all her attention on correcting it.*

No energy needs to be wasted explaining why the error was made, defending, or feeling dumb. "Oops" allows a person to "do over," and in doing it right, feel successful. Then when you see the person doing the corrected behavior, slather on the positive recognition for a happy ending.

~ 45 ~
LOOKING ON THE BRIGHT SIDE

I went to Sandy Mush, North Carolina, to visit my eighty-five-year-old mother. It was raining hard when I pulled into her driveway, so I turned the car around and backed into her carport, taking advantage of the dry shelter to unload my suitcase and the empty Tupperware cake carrier I'd brought back for a refill.

As I checked my backing progress in the side mirror of my car, I spotted Mother standing in the kitchen door, watching my slow approach. Her face lit up when I got out of the car. "You get 'a hundred' for backing in here so straight!" she announced.

I smiled and gave her a long bear hug. I hadn't known my mother's rating of my driving proficiency could give me such a lift after a tiring four-hour trip. It was the beginning of a very pleasant visit.

This sounds like such a small thing, but life is made up of small things. Years are made up of months and days, which are made up of hours and minutes. What my mother did in that fraction of a minute set the tone for the rest of the day. Who would think to make a positive comment about the way someone backed up a car? Well, my mother, that's who! Now the secret is out. You know who taught me (with her actions) all I know about positive recognition.

Commenting positively on people's actions and the situations we find ourselves in is the perfect way to look on the bright side. In fact, doing that creates a bright side for us to *look* on. This is more than just having a positive mental attitude. There's a reason why positive statements create more positive relationships.

A positive comment is more likely to evoke a positive comment by the person who hears it. It

Life is made up of small things.

"If you hold a positive thought, you cannot hold a negative thought."

—Lily Tomlin

serves as a cue for another person to "scan" for positives. They feed on themselves.

On the other side of the coin, a negative comment is likely to get a negative comment in response.

I'm sure you know people who focus on the opposite side of the moon, always looking on the dark side. Those are the folks who complain about things they or you can't control. *(Dadgum* stoplight! It stops me every time!) When things go wrong, the way they talk about the situation makes it even more unpleasant. (We're lost now. We'll never get there. I'll be late for the meeting and probably get fired for it. I won't have a paycheck and they'll repossess my house. I'll be sleeping on the streets and starving in a month's time.)

Well, go ahead and catch a cold and die, just to complete the thought.

My girlfriends, Susan and Betsy, and I checked into a hotel on the last day of a week's vacation trip, glum and exhausted. The only accommodation we could find was one room for the three of us. When we walked into the room with a week's worth of souvenirs and luggage, it was so small we didn't have enough space around the beds to set the suitcases down on the floor. Forget about tabletop space for unpacking. When we began to unpack, we had to take turns putting one suitcase at a time on the bed to take out our clothes, while the other two sat on the other daybed, waiting their turns.

The small window looked onto a grim, dirty street scene. We began to hear construction noises on the other side of the thin wall. The mattresses were uncomfortably hard even when we sat on them; we didn't want to think about what they'd feel like when we tried to sleep. Only one of the lamps had a working lightbulb. It felt hot and stuffy.

We all looked at each other and started laughing. It felt like a scene in a movie. We realized that we could either laugh or cry. Fortunately, both my friends are people who look on the bright side of all situations, so we turned a bad situation around. We began playing a little game. Someone said, "Let's go on a treasure hunt, and see how many positive things we can find about this room, if any, and name them."

Betsy said, "Well, it's close to the train station."

Susan added, "The window at least opens, so we can cool it off in here."

I brilliantly pointed out, "The walls go all the way up to the ceiling."

Susan noticed that the bathroom had been remodeled and had a shiny countertop. Betsy noted that there were three towels.

With each new observation, we giggled at what trivial things we were mentioning and how funny it was to be scraping the bottom of the "positive" barrel. Before we knew it, we were all in better moods. We freshened up, went out to dinner, and now had a funny story to tell about the end of our trip.

If nothing else, bad situations usually give us a good story to tell.

We can realize that when bad things happen, we don't have to choose to make negative statements about them. These two are separate events:

- a bad thing happens
- someone makes negative statements

The first can happen without the second following it. It's our choice.

With the points I'm making here, I don't include tragic or life-threatening situations. I'd be the last to suggest that we try to "lighten up" when someone's health or well-being is involved. Our feelings during those times shouldn't be teased. But some unhappy situations we find ourselves in won't seem so bad by the time the sun rises the next time.

Whistle while you work.

I once heard some good advice in the form of a question: "Will any of this matter five years from now? Will I even remember it?"

This seems to me to be a good test. Just asking the question helps me put problems in perspective and minimize my negative talk, whether I'm talking to other people or talking to myself.

One more story about my energetic, positive mother:

Her lifelong friend, Callie, had a grandson who was getting married on a Saturday afternoon. Lovely, engraved invitations had been sent. Parties had been enjoyed. Gifts had been given. The wedding had been rehearsed. Callie was the happiest my mother had ever seen her. The grandson was the last of her grandchildren to marry, and the bride-to-be was a young woman that everyone in the family had come to love.

But on the morning of the wedding, the grandson called it off. Stunned family members divided up the guest list and started making embarrassed phone calls. When my mother received her cancellation call, she sprang into action. She went to the store and bought ice cream, champagne, and cake. She then called Callie's home and asked permission to bring her party provisions for a visit. Callie's daughter assented. She then informed her moping family members that Pauline Allen was on her way.

When my mother arrived, she told them all that since this large, wonderful family had gathered, she thought it would be a shame to waste an opportunity for a party. No one could help but smile as this four-foot, ten-inch, eighty-year-old angel swooped down to cheer them up. It worked, of course.

Everyone heard the pop when the champagne was opened and immediately their moods changed. Then they could just enjoy the special occasion of being together.

Sandy Mush Vineyards

Bad situations at least give us a good story to tell.

I'm sure the family had sad moments later, but at least they had a "lighten-up break" to help them through it.

THE EVIL EYE

Legend has it that in old Crete, there were rules about avoiding what was called the "Evil Eye." You wear this little amulet that looks like a blue eyeball. But the main thing is, you never, ever mention anything you're proud of.

It's a horrible social error to give somebody a compliment, because you're attracting the attention of the Evil Eye. So you say everything backwards.

"When two mothers pass each other on the road carrying babies, one says to the other, 'Ugly baby!' and the other one says, 'Yours also!' "

Source: ANIMAL DREAMS by Barbara Kingsolver

XVI

Leadership

~ 46 ~
ACTING FIRST

You might be thinking, "All of these ideas sound good. What a great world it would be if everyone would just do everything recommended in this book." There are two ways to view this:

- Hope everyone else will do these things— and criticize them if they don't.
- Act first to do these things, without regard for who else is or isn't doing them.

As you make your choice, it's a good time to talk about leadership. The word leadership is used a lot. Our definition of leadership is "acting first."

Acting, of course, means doing something—the somethings suggested in these pages, for instance. Hoping, from the first choice above, isn't acting. By the way, hoping rhymes with moping.

Acting first means not waiting for anyone else. When we step out to do something first, we're at

Hoping
rhymes
with
moping.

the head of the parade. We're more concerned with what's ahead than with what's behind us. We have no time or energy to spend on people who aren't joining in the parade. Acting first means taking a risk. The risk of making changes and the discomfort that's a natural part of change.

Someone said to me, "The traffic's so bad, I wish people would start using public transportation and carpooling to get some of these cars off the road." That person, of course, wasn't using public transportation or carpooling. He was using the *hoping* method of problem solving. He had the power to make his own life easier by making one of the changes he hoped everyone else would. Ironic, isn't it?

The exemplar of leadership was Mother Teresa. She began her work by taking a basket full of bread out into the streets to feed hungry people. Someone told her, "Mother, that isn't enough bread for so many hungry people." She said, "I'll do what I can."

The shopkeepers, when they saw what she was doing, brought bread to refill her basket when it was empty. She fed many more. Her leadership, by acting first, inspired them to follow. Her religious order, the Missionaries of the Poor, now feeds hundreds of thousands around the world.

Mother Teresa didn't go out preaching to shopkeepers to try to get them to feed the hungry. Or sit at home and hope. She acted first, doing a small thing she could control, and others followed.

Go make someone's day.

Every idea in this book is for an action that you can control. You need not wait, wish, or hope other people will do these things. Instead, let them see *you* acting first. They will see you as a leader.

No one will do these things perfectly or do them consistently. I certainly don't. I can be as crabby as anyone on earth. Ask my co-author.

Fortunately, none of us have to be a Mother Teresa to make a difference.

So, go out and make someone's day!

RECOMMENDED RESOURCES

1001 Ways to Reward Employees (1994)
Bob Nelson, Workman Publishing Company, Inc.,
708 Broadway, New York, New York, 10003.

Bringing Out the Best in People (Revised Edition
1999) Dr. Aubrey C. Daniels, McGraw-Hill,
11 West 19th Street, New York, New York, 10011.

Care Packages for the Workplace (1996)
Barbara A. Glanz, McGraw-Hill,
11 West 19th Street, New York, New York, 10011.

*How to Improve Human Performance:
Behaviorism in Business and Industry* (1978)
Thomas K. Connellan, Harper & Row,
10 East 53rd Street, New York, New York, 10022.

*I Saw What You Did and I Know Who You Are:
Bloopers, Blunders, and Success Stories on Giving
and Receiving Recognition* (1990)
Janis Allen with Gail Snyder,
Performance Management Publications, Inc.
Phone: 828-862-6552. Fax: 828-862-6553.
E-mail: janisallen@yahoo.com.

*Janis Allen on Recognition: What Everyone Who
Works With People Needs to Know* (audio tape)
Janis Allen with Michael McCarthy,
Our Ownselves Publications,
1 Unutsi Court, Brevard, North Carolina, 28712.
Phone: 828-862-6552. Fax: 828-862-6553.
E-mail: janisallen@yahoo.com.

The Joy of Recognition (2000)
Lynnette Youngqren with Debra Sikanas,
Baudville, Inc. Phone: 800-728-0888.
www.baudville.com.

Performance Management: Improving Quality
Productivity Through Positive Reinforcement (1989)
Dr. Aubrey C. Daniels,
Performance Management Publications, Inc.,
3531 Habersham at Northlake,
Tucker, Georgia, 30084. Phone: 770-493-5080.

Performance Teams: Completing the Feedback
Loop (1982) Janis Allen,
Performance Management Publications, Inc.
Phone: 828-862-6552. Fax: 828-862-6553.
E-mail: janisallen@yahoo.com.

Recognition Redefined: Building Self-esteem at
Work (1992) Roger Hale and Rita Maehling,
Tennant Company,
P.O. Box 1452, Minneapolis, Minnesota, 55440-1452.

SUBJECT INDEX

NAME INDEX

For information on training, train-the-trainer workshops and other recognition books, tapes, and materials by Janis Allen and Michael McCarthy, contact janisallen@yahoo.com, phone: 828-862-6552, or Fax: 828-862-6553.

ABOUT THE AUTHORS

JANIS ALLEN has been a personnel clerk for J.P. Stevens Company, a personnel manager and corporate training director for Milliken & Company, a performance management consultant for Aubrey Daniels & Associates, and now is owner of Performance Leadership Consulting.

She helps organizations install measurement, feedback, positive-recognition systems, and performance teams. Some of the companies she has worked with are: Xerox, Blue Cross and Blue Shield, Kodak, Lebhar-Friedman, Inc., Midwest Express Airlines, United Airlines, 3M, the Department of the Army, and Eastman Chemical. She speaks to groups about positive recognition, and works with both associates and managers.

Her other books are *Performance Teams* and *I Saw What You Did and I Know Who You Are.* Janis is a jogger who likes to tease her mother and host charades parties.

MICHAEL McCARTHY has been a teacher in Key West, Florida, and aboard a sailing schooner in Europe. He was a counselor at the Eckerd Therapeutic Wilderness Camps before working as a performance management consultant with Behavioral Systems, Inc., and Aubrey Daniels & Associates. For three years he edited *Performance Management Magazine.* He has consulted in process improvement and change management. Some of the companies he has worked with are: Ford Motor Company, Preston Trucking, 3M, Kodak, and BellSouth.

Michael is a jogger and sometime martial arts student. He likes to do improvement projects around the house, read, and watch his daughter Shawn play soccer for Rhodes College.

Janis and Michael are married and they live in Brevard, North Carolina.